Grant's Getaways

Oregon Adventures with the Kids

Grant McOmie

WESTWINDS
PRESS®

Library of Congress Cataloging-in-Publication Data —

Names: McOmie, Grant.
Title: Grant's getaways : Oregon adventures with the kids / Grant McOmie.
Description: Portland, Oregon : WestWinds Press, [2017] | Includes index.
Identifiers: LCCN 2017007271 | ISBN 9781513260464 (pbk.)
Subjects: LCSH: Outdoor recreation for children—Oregon—Guidebooks. | Family
  recreation—Oregon—Guidebooks. | Oregon—Guidebooks.
Classification: LCC GV191.63 .M36 2017 | DDC 796.509795—dc23 LC record
available at https://lccn.loc.gov/2017007271

Edited by Michelle Blair and Kathy Howard
Designed by Vicki Knapton
Map by Gray Mouse Graphics and Vicki Knapton

Published by WestWinds Press®
An imprint of

GRAPHIC ARTS
BOOKS®
www.graphicartsbooks.com

For Birt Hansen—a master teacher who showed me where THE salmon live in the nooks and crannies of rivers that flow from the heart of Oregon. His friendship and guidance forever changed my course in life.

And

For my wife—Christine—my finest and favorite travel companion and the part of my life that I call happiness.

Contents

Fall

October

November

December

Winter

January

February

March

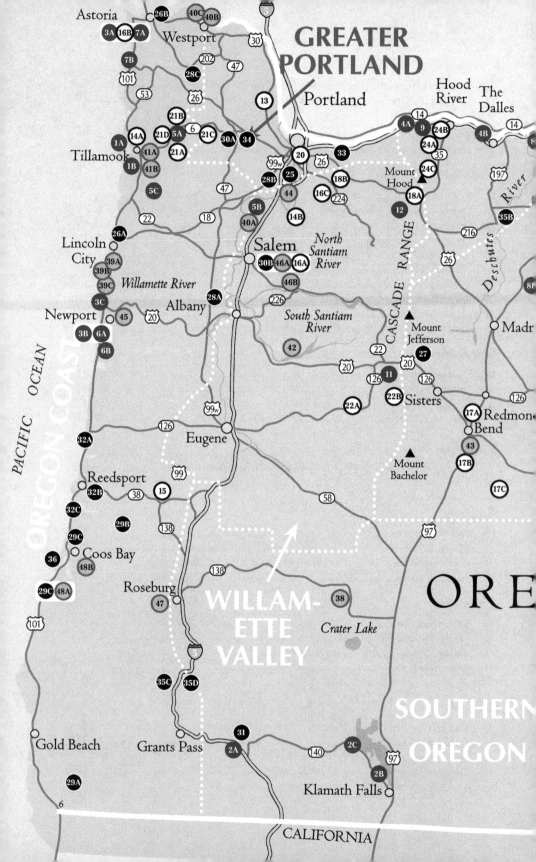

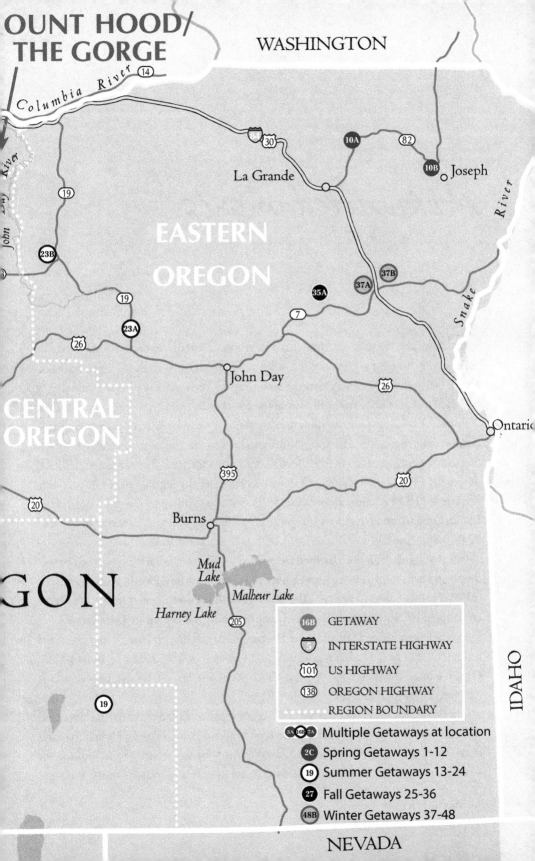

OUNT HOOD/
THE GORGE

WASHINGTON

Columbia River 14

John Day River

19

EASTERN

OREGON

23B

19

23A

26

CENTRAL
OREGON

20

GON

La Grande

34 30

10A 82

10B Joseph

Snake River

37B

37A

35A

7

John Day

26

Ontario

395

20

Burns

Mud
Lake

Malheur Lake

Harney Lake 205

19

IDAHO

16B	GETAWAY	
	INTERSTATE HIGHWAY	
101	US HIGHWAY	
138	OREGON HIGHWAY	
	REGION BOUNDARY	

3A 16B 7A Multiple Getaways at location

2C Spring Getaways 1-12

19 Summer Getaways 13-24

27 Fall Getaways 25-36

48B Winter Getaways 37-48

NEVADA

Acknowledgments

There are two words that this television outdoor reporter never—ever—wants to hear while working at some lonely outpost in the Oregon outback. I have learned the hard way that the two simple words usually portend something bad is about to derail my well-laid plans for the day and the words go like this: "Oh-ohhhhh." Let me give you an example: not so many decades ago, longtime outdoor photographer Mike Rosborough and I made the arduous trek to distant Southeast Oregon, not far from Jordan Valley, to join a 5-day rafting expedition down the Owyhee River. The Owyhee River runs through a corner of the state known as "I-O-N" country because of its close proximity to the state borders of Idaho, Oregon, and Nevada, which mesh together in a vastness covering more than 10,000 square miles.

If you mention the Owyhee to most folks, they stare back at you a tad bewildered and ask, "Did you say Ow-ya-hoo-ee? Or, Aw-ya-hay?" Well, it's pronounced "oh-WYE-hee," as in "Hawaii." The story goes that Peter Skene Ogden, who led a contingent of North West Company trappers into the region in 1819, named the Owyhee River. Three Hawaiians had been sent to trap for furs on a tributary of the Snake River, where Ogden was camped. The trappers were killed by Indians, and Ogden named the tributary for them. Over the centuries, the "Hawaii River" name has been corrupted into the "Owyhee River."

Out of the way? It certainly is! This is a most secluded and pristine river, and with the sound of its water rushing through boulder-strewn rapids, it's just the kind of territory that stirs my senses and satisfies my soul. It's where I went looking for adventure with Gerald Moore, the owner and operator of Water Otters. We were slated to float the wild Owyhee River to produce a special outdoor program. So we joined Moore's outfitting and guide company because it specialized in Oregon's hard-to-reach rivers. Also, unlike large white-water rafts that seat up to six people, Water Otters (as the name implies) offered a flotilla of small, more intimate, inflatable kayaks. It was a cozy, self-sufficient experience, where you were your own skipper on a voyage of discovery.

We met our host and his crew an hour before sunrise and made plans to travel across the desert to a special launch point that Moore had arranged for on private land. Mike and I staked out a spot with camera and tripod that would catch the sunburst of dawn and then see the long lineup of rigs and boats. It was spectacular and a scene right out of the Old West—except—no horses, but a lineup of six pickups and SUVs. Mike gave me a quick thumbs-up that he was set—and—just like in Hollywood, I yelled "action" to our team. The rose-colored dawn was perfect and as the long trail of rigs came into view, all seemed right. That's when I heard Mike utter those two fateful words: "Oh-ohhhhh." I snapped my head to the left and shot out, "Whaaaaat?" "Oh-ohhhhh," he repeated. "The camera isn't working—no power—I don't know why but you better stop the team." So with that, I sprinted across 200 yards of juniper and sage, waved my arms high overhead, and yelled "Stop, stop, stop." And they did! I explained, "We have a technical glitch and need to do this again, but let me check with Mike first." And then, a quick turn around and I sprinted back to Mike. "Well?" I asked. "Not good, not good, but I'll try a few things," said the frustrated photographer.

Two hours later, the problem was still unsolved and we realized this was going to take far more technical know-how than either of us owned. At a time before cell phones, it meant the entire team had to return back to town to find a pay phone (remember those?) to call to our engineering department who might be able to walk us through a solution. Two hours of phone conversations followed as we shuttled between engineers and news managers until it was finally determined they or we could not fix the camera. They proposed we come home while I suggested that they ship us another camera—that very night. And they did! But it meant a lengthy road trip to the Boise airport to pick it up and a return drive that ate up most of the dark night—I recall but an hour of sleep before a return to our distant desert site for a replay of the previous day's plan. We were greeted by an even more gorgeous sunrise and believe it or not, still-smiling crew members who were patiently giving the entire effort their all. And so did we! For the most part, I didn't hear those two words again—at least not on that story—and the payoff for all the struggle required to travel into the Owyhee River canyon was an escape from the hurried, harried hubbub of city life.

That's something I really noticed our second night out, when we camped across a wide apron of sand that gently kissed the river. I could feel the quiet shout at me! Surrounded by steep rock towers, I was restless and couldn't sleep. As I gazed up from my snug sleeping bag, I was stunned by a sky stuffed with stars. Moore heard me stir and whispered across our otherwise quiet group of drowsy fellow travelers: "Magnificent, huh? This float combines so much into one trip. You're rafting, you have white water, the fishing, and wildlife viewing. But this is the reason I come here." In the dark I imagined his hand sweeping across the night sky to touch the stars. "Almost a religious feeling as though you're closer to God and closer to nature. Virtually everyone I bring into this canyon feels the same way." I have never forgotten that feeling—a near childlike wonder for so much beauty in a remote country that was unmatched for its splendor and wealth of wildlife.

I have heard it said that "Our lives are but houses built of memories." If that's true—and it seems a fair mark of my life—I think people should make outdoor travel and adventures the bricks and mortar of their lives. I've tried to do that for more than 35 years as a teacher, television news reporter, and travel writer. *Grant's Getaways: Oregon Adventures with the Kids* is a visible measure of my effort, but, importantly, it is a work neither conceived nor completed alone. I like to brag that Jeff Kastner is the "best damned photographer in the outdoor TV business," for he does a superb job of capturing the finest getaway moments with his camera. His keen eye and artistic touch are satisfying and humbling to behold . . . all of which makes my story writing much, much easier.

My sincere thanks to the Travel Oregon management team for their trust and confidence in me to represent Oregon—including CEO Todd Davidson, Mo Sherifdeen, Emily Forsha, Kevin Wright, and Sachie Yorck. I also thank David Lane of the Oregon Department of Fish and Wildlife, Ashley Massey of the Oregon State Marine Board, and Chris Havel of the Oregon Parks and Recreation Department. I appreciate their insights, advice, and story suggestions. Further, I extend my deep gratitude to the KGW-TV management team including DJ Wilson, Brenda Buratti, and News Director Rick Jacobs. Each continues to embrace and encourage our work at every turn

I also thank the folks at Graphic Arts Books for the chance to continue telling my stories from the great Oregon outdoors, including Kathy Howard, Vicki Knapton, Angie Zbornik, and most especially, Michelle Blair, a superb copyeditor who corrected and improved this text a thousandfold, and more importantly researched, secured, and offers—in this book—terrific information for parents who wish to make their travel with kids an easier experience. While I enjoy the storytelling, this book would not be nearly as valuable to parents and kids without Michelle's well researched and thoughtful insights into the basics of clothing, special equipment, varied safety measures, phone numbers, and directions—the sort of bread-and-butter content that makes this work a much more useful buy. Thank you, Michelle!

As always, I thank my wife, Christine, my finest and favorite travel companion. Finally, I'll let you in on a little secret: I get a kick out of the traveling life! More so now than ever before. And I suspect you do, too, so I extend my sincere appreciation to all who find pleasure and satisfaction in the journey.

Foreword

I've had the privilege of sitting in a front-row seat on dozens of *Grant's Getaways* television adventures. As one of his regular guests, the two of us have enjoyed some remarkable adventures and several of them in the company of youngsters. Whether it was trout fishing on Henry Hagg Lake with my son or helping Eric McOmie land his first steelhead on the Cowlitz River when he was just a lad, I've watched Grant work his magic in translating these wonderful moments into memorable television segments. Those stories have fired the ambition and dreams of parents and kids around the Pacific Northwest, helping to create a new legion of outdoor enthusiasts.

A little about Grant. What you see is what you get. He's as passionate about the outdoors as you see in his regular broadcasts and he genuinely loves what he does. Who wouldn't?

Just a few months ago, we enjoyed a trip on the Columbia River with our mutual friend and professional fishing guide, John Krauthoefer. Grant hooked and landed a gorgeous, ocean-bright chinook salmon. This fish was strong, pulling line off the reel in long, dogged runs. Just when we thought we'd had this fish beat, off it would go. When we finally got it in the net, Grant sat on the gunwale of the boat with a big smile of satisfaction and said, "Look, I'm shaking!" Sure enough he was. Even after landing hundreds of salmon, Grant's excitement was real and visible. It reminded me that no matter how old we are or how often we've done something in our lives, there's a kid in all of us.

Twenty years ago, I watched Grant tame a fifth-grade class in minutes. He was making school visits around the Portland area and invited me to join him. Grant opened with a series of questions, not just any run-of-the-mill "do you spend time outdoors" questions, but ones that immediately captured the attention of the class. "What's the Oregon state bird?" A couple students raised their hands, waving in earnest, straining to be recognized. "The western meadowlark," one student blurted. "That's right, very good, let me tell you a little about the western meadowlark. . . ." Grant shared the what and why of Oregon's state bird and followed it with another series of questions that kept the kids completely engaged the entire hour of his visit. Watching it, I thought, *he's good.* He had this group in the palm of his hands in seconds. No easy feat.

Grant's desire to share his love of the outdoors with kids is part of who he is. On one of our many trips for spring chinook, we'd been trolling fruitlessly for hours. As we waited for the fish to bite, we talked about fifty different things ranging from our families to work as we mined the Willamette River for these wonderful fish. Out of nowhere, Grant asked, "You know why we love to take our kids fishing?" I must have looked like I had no clue because Grant quickly added, "Because we get to relive these experiences all over again—*through their eyes.*" He's right! That indelible conversation reshaped how I viewed those experiences and I've grown to enjoy them even more, understanding that those moments are as special for me as they are for kids.

Grant knows better than most how important it is to connect kids to the outdoors. He's seen it through his kids and those of his friends. Those grade school years are so formative and impressionable, more so than any other time in our lives. Kids remember those adventures for a lifetime. This collection of trips and adventures Grant's assembled in his latest book, *Grant's Getaways: Oregon Adventures with the Kids,* are all kid-tested and are sure to create important outdoor connections and inspire many lifetime memories. Whether it's pulling in pot loads of Dungeness crabs or catching trout or pitching a tent and sleeping under the stars, these stories are ideal getaways for the entire family. Take Grant's advice and "Get out there and enjoy the great Oregon outdoors!"

—Trey Carskadon

Introduction

N ow, Grant—tell us again, what is it that you do for a living? I hear it has something to do with the television. I don't watch a lot of TV, but I would if you were on there . . . but I don't really understand what it is you do—your mother said something about 'Grant goes fishing.'"

It felt a lot like a doubleheader baseball game that had gone terribly wrong—two pitchers throwing heat at the same time—these were fastballs with uncanny accuracy as my favorite grandmothers were trying hard for a quick "strike three and you're out" on their grandson, who, at that moment felt like scrambling into the dugout.

"Well, Grandma Sadie—Grandma Dee—it's actually not just fishing," I replied. "In fact, I travel across the entire Northwest on a variety of stories about people, places, outdoor recreation, and environmental issues for a Portland television station. They've sent me to Alaska, Canada, and most every state in the greater West—I've even traveled to Hawaii a couple of times."

"So, you get paid to go fishing?" responded Grandma Sadie, our family matriarch.

"Is that it, eh?" came a high and inside fastball query from Grandmother Dee.

I was struggling with my answers—trying to find the exact words that explained my dream job come true. It was the mid-1980s and I'd just returned to Portland from a nearly 3-year stint of work at KOMO-TV in Seattle, where I'd proven myself as the outdoor reporter for a major market television station.

"And you call that work?" came the low and away curveball inquiry from my great-grandmother Sadie, who at 98 was sharp as a tack and determined to close out the inning.

I paused for a moment to carefully consider my words so as not to hurt my grandmother's feelings. "Yes, it is work—darned hard work sometimes too," I explained. "My photographers and I work year-round—day and night, anywhere, anytime under all conditions on unique stories about Oregon," I insisted. "Try to understand, when it comes to Oregon, I'm absolutely sold on the notion that people love what they know and will protect what they love. So for me, storytelling with pictures is like a calling and anyway, I can't imagine—even after a handful of years—I can't imagine doing anything else. In fact, I don't know how to do anything else."

Suddenly, there was a hush and all was quiet on my grandmothers' side of the kitchen table—it was as though I'd just hit a grand slam that sealed the game—it was bottom of the ninth and game over!

True story!

Over the past 35 years, when it came to explaining the challenges and pleasures of my work to friends, family, or even complete strangers, I've always acknowledged a bit of gut-wrenching guilt about my explanations. It's been terrific work to be sure—but how much fun are you allowed to have—on any job? I've always been open about my unabashed love affair with my home state, one that reaches back to my earliest childhood memories of adventures with my family.

Seventeen years ago, I wrote about this love affair: "When I was a boy I fell in love with long distance—not the telephone kind, but the dust-filled lanes and rambling asphalt roads that enticed a small-town kid from central Oregon to explore his home region more than 40 years ago. These roads invited me to roam Oregon's remote alpine mountains, glacier-fed rivers, and nearly 400 miles of Pacific shoreline."

Little has changed! Quite the contrary, for as I've grown older and traveled even more, I'm also a bit wiser from the doing of the thing. Longtime newsman Charles Kuralt said it best, "I am seduced by travel!" Put me in his camp, for the love of my home state's incredible variety of geography, climate, and people has grown even deeper. I've an insatiable appetite for the new or the old and the interesting—from the smallest of Oregon's homegrown stories to the giant ones. I have been most fortunate to travel and meet new folks each week, write about the journeys and adventures, and then see the television screen come alive with stunning images and compelling stories from our travels. That love and the memories are at the root of this book—to reach back and hold on to my childhood recollections a little while longer and also relive the memories of time and place with my own sons' Oregon explorations when they were young so many years ago.

I am told that there is keen interest for *Oregon Adventures with the Kids* and I'm hoping you will find some fresh ideas for your family's consideration here—ideas that you may have missed from our *Grant's Getaways* segments that you see on television or online. For example, you and your kids will enjoy a fishing trip on the Lake Born of Fire: Clear Lake—the headwaters of the McKenzie River where no motors are allowed and where the water is so clear you can see an entire underwater forest that was trapped by a lava flow thousands of years ago. Perhaps your kids will experience the sheer joy that comes with Two Tickets to Ride onboard scale model trains that run each summer at the Molalla Train Park—it's where the kids can be railroad engineers for the day. We also travel far afield to the distant Southeast Oregon desert and show you where and how the kids can dig what some call "drops of honey": sunstones, the Oregon state gem.

Some of our kids' getaway ideas are from earlier *Grant's Getaways* books, but have proven timeless and remain some of the most popular and requested ideas for families. Speaking of family, I'm a big believer that families who play together, stay together and this book offers many ideas perfectly suited to kids and adults alike. For example, when you step aboard Marine Discovery Tours you'll learn much about the marine life that lives in Yaquina Bay at Newport. Or take a ride together on a Zip-a-Dee-Doo-Dah zip line—I offer two zip line rides and each will take your breath away as you fly through the forests. We also meet a man whose invention takes the strain out of digging razor clams: The King of the Clam Gun has come up with a special design for kids to help them enjoy the recreation right beside the adults. Your family will want to seek out the unique and ancient Oregon hoodoos—there's nothing else quite like them at one of the state's most popular recreation areas in Central Oregon. If you're new to the Oregon territory and have an interest in camping, paddling, crabbing, or any number of other outdoor recreation activities, we'll set you on the right course with the Oregon Parks and Recreation Department's Let's Go programs that specialize in teaching newcomers the ropes.

I also offer parents the basics to introduce their youngsters to varied outdoor activities—the clothing, the gear, and the safety measures you should know about and the required equipment you should bring with you when you head out. The book spans the varied geophysical regions of the state and includes adventures for each month of the year. I have selected locations and stories and tips and tactics that will guide you and especially the kids to forty-eight of my favorite destinations during what I consider their seasonal peaks. These are places I have especially enjoyed at a particular time of year. But let me be clear: These are but my preferred times to visit, so don't get the notion they don't shine at other times of the year.

My getaway selections offer my favorite experiences that have kept my pho-

Chris and I always made sure the kids joined us in the Oregon outdoors. Jackson Bottom Wetlands (circa 1999). Photo courtesy of Steve Terrill.

tographers on their toes through the decades. Many of the destinations are accessible on a tank of gas, while others require more planning and time. Throughout the book I use sidebars to describe interesting bonus trips as well as more in-depth educational information and detailed travel strategies, extra content that I'm not able to share during my weekly television programs. I mention wheelchair accessibility where available, although there is almost always a path or trail nearby that can be navigated in a wheelchair. Each getaway concludes with contact names, phone numbers, and websites for further information.

Much of my personal interest in your success with the kids comes from my background as a public school teacher; a passion to impart knowledge and skills comes naturally for a fellow whose classroom simply got much bigger through the years. It has always been my greatest hope that viewers or readers learn something new when they watch our stories or read my books. Moreover, I want more youngsters outdoors, enjoying Oregon. The more they experience, the more they learn and the more they learn, the more respect they embrace for what Oregon represents—and with respect grows a desire to help make our state a better place.

Finally, the point of all this, as I like to tell folks in person, on the air, or in writing, is just to get out there, enjoy Oregon any time of year, and make some memories of your own. I hope my *Oregon Adventures with the Kids* will guide your way.

Spring

Grant McOmie's Outdoor Talk— Three for the Price of One Getaway

"D ad, I mean it. There's something or someone out there by the picnic table! I can hear it," whispered my youngest son, Kevin, whose flashlight shone wildly through the small trailer window and across the campsite, like some out-of-kilter lighthouse beacon.

"Kev, I don't hear anything," I consoled him. "And there's nothing out there to be bothering anyway. So turn off the light—you're burning up the batteries. Roll over and go to sleep before you wake your brothers and mom—big day tomorrow."

In fact, that day had been a very big day for us: a rite-of-spring-break passage my family enjoyed each March when the five of us become a family on the move, bound for new adventures and new places to see. We were never ones to let the grass grow under our feet when we took our home on the road; instead, we were outdoors building lasting memories like the ones I have long cherished from my own childhood travels across the Pacific Northwest.

So it was at midnight, on this first day of a spring break, that we'd finished a 5-hour drive from our Forest Grove homesite, arrived at Sunset Bay State Park in Coos County, Oregon, and quietly tried to slip into the first of many vacation slumbers.

Kevin and I shared the fold-out dining table (now a turned-down overnight twin bed) and, like most wiggly 10-year-olds, he was wired with excitement on the eve of our vacation, stretching and squirming before finding just the right spot to dive into sleep land. Suddenly his ever-ready flashlight beamed at my eyeballs to signal he was awake, alarmed, and at attention for unseen whatevers rambling outside.

"But, Dad. . . ."

"Now, Kev, we don't want—" My speech about getting enough sleep for the next day's adventures was cut short by an unmistakable and loud raking of animal claws across metal. It, or whatever it might be, was scratching on the trailer door.

"I told ya," Kevin quickly whispered, head ducking down into his sleeping bag like a wounded turtle, snug in the protection of his down shell. I rolled over and out (little choice when a child's elbow meets your midsection) and was airborne, then dumped onto the shaking floor of our 20-foot travel trailer. The entire family was immediately grasping for consciousness and gasping from fright—and not very happy about the early wake-up call either.

"It's, uhh, a someone . . . or a something . . . maybe a critter or . . . uhh, sorry," I groaned while stumbling, bumping, finding balance then focus—and finally my pants.

At the door I quickly turned the lock loose, then slowly worked the metal L-shaped handle down and cracked the door open with my right hand. I had Kev's light saber in my left hand, and as I slowly tilted it downward, two of the brightest beacons of reflected light I'd ever seen glowed back at me.

"It's a raccooooooon," Kevin cooed, "a cutey, too. Look, Dad. He's standing on his back legs—like he's begging or something, like he's hungry, huh?"

Now campsite raccoons are not a bit unusual given the current state of affairs in many rural communities or parks (and even most urban settings) whenever kindhearted summer visitors leave scraps of burgers, buns, chips, or even dog food out all night. But this was a first—a raccoon shopping for midnight snacks at our RV, a critter making a wildlife house call.

"What do we do?" the rest of the clan wondered aloud. Kev's plan came on the heel of their question: "Give him whatever he wants—look at those teeth. He's grinning at us . . . or smiling . . . or something. Can a raccoon be happy, Dad?"

"Well, I suppose if he's got enough to eat he's happy—and this one looks all of 30 or 40 pounds, so I'd say he's real happy—maybe 50 pounds' worth of happiness. That's one of the biggest, boldest raccoons I've ever seen. And he's overjoyed that he's got new neighbors who may share more than a cupful of sugar. But I don't think sharing is the thing to do—once we start, he'll be back again and again—and I'm not crazy about these middle-of-the-night meals, so let's close the restaurant and stay closed. Besides—"

"Here, boy!" Eric's right fist poked through the opened doorway and released its prize: a 6-inch slab of beef jerky he'd been hoarding from earlier in the day.

Now that raccoon may have been huge as a house, but it was also lightning quick, snapping up the beef chunk in midair as smoothly and effortlessly as a breezy major-league move to a fly ball blasted to center field.

And with that I closed the door! But I swear—just before latch met frame, like some furry Buddha with a knowing nod—that raccoon winked, smiled, and waved at me before waddling across the campground to meet our nearest neighbor.

This chapter of the "wild" life at Sunset Bay State Park notwithstanding, I am thrilled with each visit to this region. You actually get three state parks for the price of one vacation: Sunset Bay, Shore Acres, and Cape Arago State Parks are within 2 miles of each other and connected by road, bike trail, and hiking path. Each park serves up a distinctive flavor of the southern Oregon coastline.

Sunset Bay is a small overnight campground, with sixty-six tent sites, sixty-three trailer sites, and eight yurts. The park also features a hiker/biker camp, plus two group tent camps. Hot showers and flush toilets are available to all campers and provide a welcome comfort zone. There's plenty of elbow room and trails to explore across the park's 20 acres—especially along Big Creek, which flows for a half mile through the heart of the forested campground into the namesake bay.

Thomas Hirst, an early settler in Coos Bay, named Sunset Bay when it was used by fishing boats and other shallow vessels as a protective harbor during violent storms. But I feel the wind-shorn, wave-battered cliffs hint of some far-off shore—say, Polynesia? Or Alaska? Legend has it Sunset Bay was also used by pirates, and a glance toward the ocean suggests the reason: The small bay is set inside steep sandstone bluffs and has a narrow passage to the sea that's difficult to discern from the ocean.

My first visit to Shore Acres State Park—Oregon's only botanical garden, a mile south of Sunset Bay—is shrouded in a foggy mist that time often lends to an adult's childhood memories. I couldn't have been more than 6 or 7, but I remember wandering and then wondering who in the world pulled the weeds and mowed the 7 acres of endless green grass. (You see, this was my duty at home, so I always turned an envious eye to manicured yards in well-groomed neighborhoods.)

No tent? No RV? No problem! Rent a yurt at Sunset Bay State Park.

Shore Acres, built in 1906, was once a private estate famed for gardens of flowering trees, plants, and shrubs brought from around the world aboard the sailing ships of pioneer lumberman and shipbuilder Louis B. Simpson, as well as a 1-acre pond and shimmering waterfall. Simpson developed the summer home into a showplace capped by the towering presence of a three-story mansion. The grounds originally contained 5 acres of formal gardens, but fire destroyed the mansion in 1921. Simpson began to build an even larger replacement; however, financial losses caused both house and grounds to fall into disrepair in the 1930s. The State of Oregon purchased Shore Acres as a park in 1942.

Although the mansion had to be demolished, the restored gardens are a treasure open for your exploration, and if you're lucky you may cross paths with retired park horticulturist/ranger George Guthrie. He's the man with the green thumb who made the day-to-day operational decisions, as well as the long-term landscaping plans for the gardens.

Whether tulips, rhodies, or roses, this slightly built but enthusiastic gentleman can rattle off more botanically correct names than I might after a year of intense study. Guthrie always has a moment to sit and visit, too, and I recently asked him about the challenge of maintaining more than 15,000 plants across the 7-acre park.

"We try to create an inviting, lovely place at all times of the year, so that anyone who steps in here, even in January or February, will see something pretty and blooming," he told me. "But we also want to be a place of learning and education, and I think that's part of the entire state parks goal—to preserve beautiful places in the State of Oregon and make them accessible on a variety of levels—not just for looking but learning, too."

A short but easy 1-mile hike south takes you to Cape Arago, famous as a resort for Steller sea lions. Well, perhaps *resort* is a bit of a stretch, but the fact is that Shell Island (adjacent to the cape) is the largest Steller haul-out and calving site along the entire West Coast. It is critical habitat for these federally protected, endangered marine mammals that can weigh more than a ton.

Any time is a fine time to visit the many viewpoints along Cape Arago's main hiking path overlooking Shell Island, but keep in mind that the offshore rocks, islands, and reefs are part of the Oregon Islands National Wildlife Refuge system, which is closed to public access.

So here's a tip: Bring binoculars or a spotting scope so you'll have a front-row seat into the refuge proper and a chance to view fascinating wildlife behaviors. My favorite time to visit is April through June when sea lion young are born and begin their first tentative moves from sand to sea.

I try to make this collection of wonderful parks a 3- or 4-day stay—I like to linger and just loaf around the trails, viewpoints, and colorful gardens that this unique Oregon destination offers.

Like my good friend, retired Sunset Bay Park Ranger Andy LaTomme said, "What we find with a lot of folks is that once they come, they revisit time and time again because it is so special. Around every corner, over every little rise, there's something to delight your senses—it's a delightful place, a great place to be."

April

1

Bayocean—
A Spit You Can't Resist

Some Oregon back roads reach into the distant past, but if you join the right people—the past comes to life! I love the kind of travel that puts me in touch with adventure—especially when it intersects with the Pacific Coast Scenic Byway—that promises to teach me more about Oregon's past.

Bayocean is a spit you cannot resist. Drive west from the town of Tillamook to reach Bayocean Road, which skirts the southern end of Tillamook Bay. Soon, you'll come face-to-face with the site of Bayocean Peninsula Park, a now-extinct community that was a developer's dream turned homeowner's nightmare.

Construction of the subdivision began in the early 1900s when it was coined "the Atlantic City of the West." It boasted homes, cabins, restaurants, and stores, even a centerpiece hotel with an indoor swimming pool.

Harold Bennett and Perry Reeder—now in their seventies, were boys when Bayocean was still a thriving community. Each remembers paved streets, sidewalks, and store fronts. "At one of the stores there was a famous sign taped on the window," said Bennett. "'Watch Bayocean Grow' and it was there until the time that they burned and bulldozed the building down."

Reeder said the trouble was that this sprawling concept was "built upon sand—and sand is vulnerable to wind and tides. To put it simply, sand moves!"

That's what happened after Tillamook Bay's North Jetty was completed in 1917. The Bayocean Spit began to erode within 3 years following the jetty's construction.

Between 1932 and 1950, the ocean cut a mile-long swath across the spit and across the townsite. Slowly at first and then with greater momentum, homes began

Bayocean's Dance Hall (foreground) burned down while the natatorium slid into the sea by 1939.

to slip and slide into the deep blue sea. "Buildings were falling down, houses were going into the ocean, and people had to move out. It was all so sad," said longtime Cape Meares resident Barbara Bennett.

She remembers homes sliding down eroding sand dunes: "Many people lost their lots, their houses, and their money and were able to save only their possessions."

Reeder added, "It's really amazing how well the people took it—if it happened today there would be lawsuits everywhere, but those people stand out in my mind—they took it so well."

Some homes were saved from ruin when they were moved. Like the one that is nicknamed the "Pagoda House" for its distinct style. "It was falling off a hill and they had to pull it through a sandy area with tractors until they could get it on a truck," said Jerry Sutherland.

Sutherland is a history buff who is fascinated by the Bayocean story. He devotes a blog to the saga (bayocean.net) and writes about the community regularly and said that five homes and the Bayocean School were moved to the nearby village of Cape Meares in the nick of time.

In fact, the former Bayocean Elementary School was remodeled and now serves as the Cape Meares Community Center. "It was a case of nature against man and nature didn't care much about what happened to the people—it just got worse and worse until the community was burned and bulldozed under in the 1950s," said Sutherland. The public is welcome to visit the community center, but its hours of operation are irregular, so check in with the building managers through the association website before your trip.

Still, Bennett and Reeder hold on to their shared history and childhood memories by placing signs and markers across the spit to show where the roads ran and where the many stores and hotels stood. Both fellows are proud to have been a part of a community that was once a vacation destination and is still open for exploration—on foot or on bike. In fact, you can rent bikes with fat tires customized for riding on the sand. Today, Bayocean Spit is managed as a Tillamook County Park and the marked sites are open for you and your kids to visit anytime. It is great fun to stroll its 4-mile length even though all signs of the former community are long gone.

1A Bayocean Peninsula Park

Where: Bayocean Dike Road just north of Cape Meares State Park
Web: co.tillamook.or.us/gov/Parks
Phone: 503-322-3477

1B Bayocean School (now Cape Meares Community Center)

Where: 5690 4th Street NW, Tillamook, OR 97141
Web: Cape Meares Community Association (owner of the old
    Bayocean School): capemeares.org
Watch the Episode: traveloregon.com/bayocean-spit

2

Zip-a-Dee-Doo-Dah at Oregon Zip Lines

W hen I was a boy—say, 10 or 11—I lived for after-school free time—up in the trees! Really! I was a tree climber and my heart soared with each reach up into the giant Doug fir trees that bordered our backyard—the giants were like a haven to a kid who loved to really "get away from it all." Other neighborhood kids my age did the same and some of the lucky ones even had tree forts that allowed us to spread sleeping bags, light a lantern, and spend the night.

Perhaps that's why I have a newfound love affair with a popular recreation that is spreading across Oregon like wildfire: zip-lining, where you climb up onto platforms and soar across the skyline from one station to the next. I like to cry "Zip-a-Dee-Doo-Dah" at the top of my voice as I scream above or through the trees at two new zip line courses that are open to kids of all ages.

ROGUE VALLEY ZIPLINE

The sound gives it away—a distinct whirring and metallic noise as a dozen steel rollers spin across a thick cable. It's a high-wire act that lets you glide over tree tops and leave all your troubles behind on a Rogue Valley ZipLine Adventure. It's a ride that requires you gear up for safety so zip line guides Steve Carlino and Katie Fawkes show you the ropes of handling a harness and helmet before leading you up a short trail to ZipLine #1.

As we walked toward the first zip line, called Bunny Hop, which offers new-comers a short practice ride to get the feel of the flight, Carlino, a 10-year zipping veteran, was sporting a beaming smile and said, "Our biggest rule for the day is to have fun guys!" It's hard not to have a blast when you ride across 2,700 feet of high-wire zip lines through and above scrub oak and pine in the arid climate of Jackson County—just outside Gold Hill, Oregon.

As our small troop of zippers, led by Fawkes, rode the practice run without a slip, she said, "OK—the easy part is done—now we zip above the canopy of trees and enjoy the views we were talking about earlier. Welcome to Southern Oregon!" The zipping speed can reach 50 miles an hour or more—Carlino said that's a fact not lost on some first-timers: "We do get some folks who are a bit nervous about both speed and height. They'll say, 'I don't know if I want to do this,' but by end of the run they say, 'Wow, let's get going. I want more.'"

Each of the lines (they are numbered one to five and get progressively longer and higher) allows the zippers to gain more and more confidence. Fawkes said she loves it when she hears the zippers scream: "I do—because I know they are out of their comfort zone. I was out of my comfort zone when I first tried it too, but that's when amazing things happen. I grew and gained more confidence. I've been guiding here ever since!"

Rogue Valley ZipLine Adventure is the brainchild of owner Lindsey Rice—who zipped her first high wire in Hawaii. As she flew through the air above Oahu, she thought: "We've got better views back in Oregon!" So 8 years ago she built Rogue Valley ZipLine Adventure across the 83 wooded acres that she owned. The longest zip line is over a quarter mile long and takes advantage of something special: "Oh, it's all about the views—they are beautiful," noted Rice. "You look down and across to both the Upper and Lower Table Rocks, you can see Mt. McLoughlin and even the rim of Crater Lake." Newcomer Jessica Sites agreed and offered, "I almost wish I could have stopped in the middle of the last run to admire the scenery . . . sort of hang out for a bit and check it out—it was gorgeous."

There's more: Rogue Valley ZipLine Adventure is open to nearly everyone! "We are ADA-friendly," said Rice. "We do whatever we can to accommodate all folks who come out. They may be in wheelchairs or they may be blind—even grandmothers in their nineties can go zipping with their grandkids. We encourage the entire family to come out and enjoy this fun activity together." Note that children must be at least 8 years old, weigh a minimum of 65 pounds, and be in good physical condition. Riders aged 8 to 13 must also be accompanied by an adult chaperone. Drinks and snacks are available for purchase at their general store (water is available throughout the park) and they even have lockers to stow your gear. Allow 2½ to 3½ hours for the whole adventure.

CRATER LAKE ZIPLINE

When you travel to Klamath County in Southern Oregon, there are three words you must remember: *Just—Let—Go!* If you do, you will leave all your troubles behind! Visitors to the southern end of Oregon who pull in to the Running Y Ranch will discover a unique mix of residential development as well as fine hotel accommodations that spread across thousands of acres with stunning views to Upper Klamath Lake. The hotel rooms are generously sized and comfortable for a weekend stay, according to hotel manager and Running Y Ranch resident George Lusk: "A room with a king-sized bed and a view to either the golf course or our small village, but really you are looking at foothills, pine trees, and beautiful aspens across thousands of acres." The Running Y Ranch is located 8 miles from Klamath Falls and the locals like to boast it is the "Sunshine City" of Oregon; it offers more than 300 days of sunny skies a year! The resort's sports center provides facilities for family-friendly activities including tennis, basketball, swimming, pickleball, fitness classes, arcade games, seasonal activities for youth, and much more. And right next door in the winter months at the Bill Collier Community Ice Arena, your family can enjoy skating, broomball, and curling (minimum age varies depending on the activity).

The Running Y Ranch is a fine base camp for all sorts of outdoor recreation, especially golf on the only Arnold Palmer–designed golf course in the state. Weather permitting, a cleverly designed mini-golf putting course is fun for kids and grown-ups alike; allow an hour to play a full round. Lusk added the Running Y also boasts miles of hiking trails, canoe paddling, and wildlife watching: "Just a beautiful place to walk! It's about 2½ miles of a nature walk right along the shore of Klamath Lake. Starting in December we'll have the eagles migrate here and stay through the winter—hundreds of eagles will arrive and it's just unbelievable to see so many in one place." Your family can join thousands of birding enthusiasts who visit the Klamath

Safety is everything on a zip line and includes a helmet and harness.

Basin each year. You could even plan to join in the fun of the annual Winter Wings Festival (winterwingsfest.org) that includes several family activities.

Other visitors are eager to visit the Running Y to sign up for something new: the chance to soar through the trees at the new Crater Lake Zipline. First opened in September 2015, all you need is a harness, a helmet, and a spirit of adventure and you are smack in the middle of a forest canopy. Crater Lake Zipline is the vision of Darren and Jennifer Roe, owners of Roe Outfitters, who wanted to offer visitors something that's a bit daring, a bit challenging, and a whole lot of fun. The zip line—Oregon's eighth, but the first east of the Cascades crest—has nine long, fast lines extending from the hilltop, a pair of swinging suspension bridges, and a couple of rappels, including a short free-fall at the conclusion of the run. From each platform, views extend across the colorful marshlands of Upper Klamath, the state's largest lake. The 3-hour experience, Darren said, has already shown itself to be far more popular than he ever imagined it would be. Participating children must be at least 10 years old and weigh a minimum of 70 pounds. Lockers aren't provided, so leave valuables at home or locked out of sight in your car's trunk. Also, cameras and cell phones are not permitted, but the rangers will capture the experience on camera for you and those photos will be available for purchase at the end of your adventure.

Zip-lining is the newest but hardly the only recreational pursuit in the Klamath Falls area. Roe Outfitters itself has solo and tandem kayaks, canoes, and stand-up paddleboards available for rent. Three separate scenic areas, including the Wood River, which feeds Agency Lake on the north side of Upper Klamath, and Spring Creek, a Williamson River feeder near Collier State Park, have been designated for tours. Zip liners can also combine two adventures into Roe's "Skyak" day, which couples a morning on the wires with an afternoon of kayaking in the serene Malone Springs area in the Upper Klamath National Wildlife Refuge. This combo trip is reserved for those 10 and older, but Roe Outfitters also conducts paddleboarding adventures and hunting trips (minimum age 8) and fishing trips for families with children as young as 4. Fly-fishing trips are also available for families whose children are a minimum of 8 to 12 years old, depending on the location and type of fish. All excursions require that children are accompanied by a responsible adult. Trips through the marsh-lined channels of the Upper Klamath wetlands are far more than physical exercise. They are also exercises in wildlife watching, not only for that of the four-legged variety. In fact, the Klamath Basin is world-renowned as a bird-watching destination.

"It's the original ecotour," noted Darren. "It's the greenest thing out there and it's just a lot of fun." Seven years ago, Jen and Darren fell in love with zip-lining while on vacation and they wondered: couldn't they do something like it near their home in Klamath County. According to Jennifer, they searched the entire Oregon countryside for just the right property but discovered there's "no place like home." "A good friend of ours said, 'Hey, did you ever consider Tomahawk Ski Bowl?' And I said, 'No, but let's go take a look.'" The Roes really liked what they saw of the defunct community ski area that opened in the 1950s but then closed in the mid-1980s. They spent 2 years turning the old ski site into their zip line course, the longest in Oregon.

The nine routes total a mile and a half and you are in the trees the entire time. Darren said that the spacious views of the surrounding countryside really set Crater Lake Zipline apart. "I can't get enough of it: we have views to the mountains, to Klamath Lake—plus we are in these amazing giant trees that just take your breath away." Jennifer quickly added, "You see Klamath Lake from just about every platform of the course and it is huge—some 30 miles long and it is the biggest natural lake west of the Mississippi River."

As for the namesake, Crater Lake—Jen noted that the zip line course is just 30 minutes south of the entrance to the national park so they are a "gateway" of sorts to the park and they offer high adventure that is a fine complement to anyone's visit to Crater Lake National Park. The zipping experience is positively exhilarating as you speed along cables and reach 30 miles per hour—in fact, two of the zips are more than 1,400 feet long.

Darren said that zip lining also makes folks stronger. "We have watched people's reactions and it is amazing how much the zipping experience empowers people. We are proud of that—especially if it helps people overcome fears of heights or of trying something new." Jennifer added: "Our guests will come off of the 3-hour long course experience sporting mile-wide smiles and they will say, 'It was so much better than I expected—I feel more confident because I faced a fear and overcame it.' That's when I say, 'Yay, we built it and now people love it.' I am proud of our efforts." You will love it too! The Crater Lake Zipline is open mid-April through October.

2A Rogue Valley ZipLine Adventure

Where: Pickup location at Laurel Hill Golf Course, 9450 Old Stage Road, Central Point, OR 97502

Web: rvzipline.com

Phone: 541-821-ZIPN (9476)

Watch the Episode: TravelOregon.com/Highwire

(cont'd next page)

2B Running Y Ranch

Where: 5500 Running Y Road, Klamath Falls, OR 97601
Web: runningy.com
Phone: 541-850-5500

Roe Outfitters

Where: 5391 Running Y Road, Klamath Falls, OR 97601
Web: roeoutfitters.com
Phone: 541-884-3825

2C Crater Lake Zipline

Where: 29840 Highway 140 West, Klamath Falls, OR 97601
Web: craterlakezipline.com
Phone: 541-892-9477
Watch the Episode: traveloregon.com/CraterLakeZip

Zip-lining with Children

Zip-lining is exciting but your tour manager will put safety first. Maximize your experience by dressing for both safety and comfort—avoid baggy or loose clothing and items such as scarves. Tank tops and especially short shorts may not be a comfortable option with the required harness; closed-toe shoes are a must. Pull back longer hair into a braid or ponytail. Dress in layers for unpredictable weather. Make sure your children don't have loose items in their pockets that might disappear into the forest below. If your child wears glasses, consider a retaining cord to keep them safely in place. Call ahead for reservations and remember that your zip line hosts have prepared staff and equipment based on the number of people designated in your group, so children (or adults) who have last-minute second thoughts about participating may not be entitled to a refund. Be sure to check each company's policy before committing to participation.

TIP

3

Crazy for Crab

Each winter, commercial Dungeness crab season is red-hot and rolling despite cold, wet, and harsh weather conditions. Dean Ellsworth said his 44-foot fishing boat, the *Nola K,* is his home away from home at this time of year. Ellsworth and his three-man crew spend long days and nights tossing out and pulling in nearly a thousand 80-pound crab pots during a fishing season that begins each December in time for the holidays. "The crab season means a lot to us," noted Ellsworth—a longtime crab fisherman who began fishing more than 45 years ago. "Frankly, hundreds of people work on boats or in canneries and the crab season is a critical part of small town economies."

Dungeness crab commercial fishing season opens each December and seafood processor Steve Fick explained it's quite a catch for consumers as hundreds of pounds of fresh crab are off-loaded from fishing boats into totes at his business, Fishhawk Fisheries, in Astoria. "This is the state's most valuable seafood worth nearly 50 million-dollars to coastal communities. It's an economic component that fills a big void from December to March for many fishermen and their families who live here, plus the infrastructure of support—like the crab pot businesses or the marine supply stores—all of that business stays in our community and it is key to the viability of rural life along the Oregon coast."

Recreational crab fishing can be done year-round at the Oregon coast either by boat or from a dock. Dock crabbing requires less gear, but anyone age 12 and older will need a shellfish license in either case. Rental equipment is available from many marinas and tackle shops along the coast and you can even find shops that will cook the fresh crab for you. The Oregon Department of Fish and Wildlife website offers instructions and tips for both types of crabbing (dfw.state.or.us/mrp/shellfish/crab) and they also host crabbing classes—see the sidebar on pages 38–39 for more information.

Fick first explored the Columbia River estuary as a kid, so he knows his way around the vast waterway where the river meets the sea. We left the snug harbor of Hammond, Oregon, near Astoria and slowly motored the short distance downriver to an area just off Clatsop Beach. Fick had prepared five large crab pots or traps with varied baits—a strategy he often uses so to "see what the crabs prefer." Sometimes he'll use turkey legs, chicken wings, shad, or salmon carcasses—even a can of tuna for crab bait. Anyone say, lunchtime?

"Oh yes, a can of tuna fish is perfect bait," exclaimed Fick. "All you do is perforate the can so that the scent comes out—you can also buy canned sardines or mackerel too—both work well. As long as they have a high oil content, it seems to fish well—the scent is what draws the crab into the pot." Each Oregon crabber over age 12 must carry an Oregon Department of Fish and Wildlife Shellfish License and is allowed to use up to three crab pots. We timed our trip to fish our traps during the last hour of the incoming tide and then through the high slack tide period, which is often the best crabbing time.

Fick said it's the safest time to crab in the estuary: "There is no reason to be out here on the ebb tide—that's the outgoing tide and things can go from bad to worse in a heartbeat. It can be the most dangerous part of the tide cycle and this river can change so fast. You just don't take chances out here." Fick said that each trap should soak for 15 to 20 minutes—that allows enough time for the crabs to locate the bait and enter the pot. Each crabber is allowed a dozen male crabs apiece and in Oregon they must be 5¾ inches across the back. Females are protected to preserve the breeding population of crabs. A crab gauge or other measuring device is essential gear since some crabs miss the mark by only a fraction of an inch.

Fick and I soon had our hands full of 24 fresh crabs, and then we joined a couple of his fishing friends, Steve Williams and Terry Hartil, who love to eat fresh crab as much as they like to catch them. The trio met to prepare three of their favorite crab recipes at an annual crab fest where they share new recipes with friends and family. Each recipe also offered a low-calorie approach.

Recipe #1 is an easy-to-fix Dungeness Crab Dip. Combine ½ cup each of low-fat mayo and low-fat sour cream and 1 cup plain yogurt. Fick said he will cut the calories by 70 percent using this low-fat approach. "It is a real simple dip emphasizing low calories so you can eat this without feeling bad about it." He seasoned the dip with a tablespoon each of parsley, green onions, 1 teaspoon each of ground

The best crab bait is the freshest and includes chicken wings, shad, salmon carcasses, or tuna.

pepper and paprika—plus a tablespoon of dry ranch dressing—then he folded in 2 cups of cracked Dungeness crab. He placed the bowl of crab dip on a platter and surrounded it with varied vegetables. He added cracked crab legs across the top of the dip to provide a fine finishing touch.

"The crab is really excellent quality so this will be delicious," added Fick with a smile.

Crab recipe #2 follows the same low-calorie theme and it is called Salmon Wrapped Crab. Fick cut thin strips from a salmon fillet—each strip was approximately 6 to 7 inches long and 2 inches wide. The thin-cut salmon strips provided a base for a tablespoon of crab mix. For the mix, Fick blended 1 cup low-fat mayonnaise with 2 tablespoons each of finely chopped yellow peppers and finely chopped onion, plus 1 cup of crabmeat. He rolled up the salmon strip around the crab mix and poked a toothpick through the salmon to hold it all together. The Salmon Wrapped Crab went under the oven broiler for 2½ minutes—then he added a pinch of Parmesan cheese atop each wrap and placed the tray back under the broiler for another minute and a half. "The key," Fick cautioned, "is not to cook the fish too long or it will dry out."

Crab recipe #3 found Steve Williams and Terry Hartil outdoors on a rainy winter's night where they cooked up a Dungeness Crab Feast. Williams began by placing corn on the cob—each ear is wrapped in foil—atop the barbecue grill. (He used a Weber-style grill with white-hot charcoal for heat.) "You may not want to do this on a rainy night, but certainly in the summertime. Everyone I know loves a fresh ear of barbecued corn," he said. Williams also grilled an assortment of vegetables as a side dish for the Crab Feast that included sliced yellow squash, green zucchini, sliced peppers, asparagus spears, and red onions. Williams loves to grill oysters as a fine complement to the crab. He placed whole oysters in the shell atop the grill and closed the lid until the oysters started to pop open (about 10 minutes) and he then dabbed a small amount of butter and cooked bacon inside each oyster.

Meanwhile, Hartil placed cooked crab sections atop the Weber grill: "You're not trying to cook it again—it's already been cooked. All you want to do is warm it back up and you can add smoky flavor to it with wood chips. After 2 to 3 minutes it comes out warm and delicious."

Hartil is co-owner of Bell Buoy Seafood in Seaside and said that a Dungeness Crab Feast is a long Oregon custom: "People just love this crab! It's a coastal tradition to do this in the winter too. You can't believe the number of people who come in and say, 'When I was a little kid, my dad and grandpa brought me into the store and they bought dozens of crabs. We put them out on a table for a traditional crab feed every year.'"

Soon it was assembly time on a table jammed with the varied dishes—plus, Oregon wines and brews. I asked Steve Williams what he enjoyed the most: cooking the crab with new recipes or eating the crab once the recipe is complete. "Boy, that's a tough one," he said with a chuckle. "Let's call it a toss-up, cuz I love everything out here—that's a tough choice." The crowd that turned out for this special crab cooking segment was in heaven!

Guest diner Kerry Harsin said he'd never tried barbecued crab: "Never— and it is different. You do get a little smoky flavor and I like that—it's really good." Guest diner Shannon Dotson loved the salmon wraps and planned to make them at home. "This is amazing," said Dotson. "And so easy to make!" She admitted she wasn't a big crab eater, but that's going to change: "It's great—I've never blended crab with salmon but this is delicious."

"Dungeness crab meals can be real social events," said Fick. "Really a nice way of bringing people together—everyone at the table picking at their food and socializing." And the best part is that the recipes are so easy, anyone can try and that's something to consider while Dungeness crab is in season.

It was a perfect way to round out our crabbing adventure and bring the day's activity full circle: from the estuary to the dining table. Interestingly, Fick added that 80 percent of the crab is caught in the first month of the season—it's also the time when prices for the seafood are at their lowest. Plus, even if you don't sport fish for crab, the annual commercial crabbing season provides fresh Oregon Dungeness in your local grocery. As we enjoyed a very filling seafood dinner, I asked Fick what he liked most about the adventure that's just off his front doorstep: "Oh, it's simple to do and everyone can be involved in it. It's easy to catch a dozen crabs per person with lots of action for kids. And—you never really know until you pull the pot up what you got and that is fun!"

3A Clatsop Spit (north end of Fort Stevens State Park)

Where: 100 Peter Iredale Road, Hammond, OR 97121
Web: oregonstateparks.org
Phone: 503-861-3170 x21; 800-551-6949

3B South Beach State Park

Where: 5044 Oregon Coast Highway, South Beach, OR 97366
Web: oregonstateparks.org
Phone: 800-551-6949; 541-867-7451

3C Yaquina Bay/South Beach Marina

Where: SE Marine Science Drive and US Highway 101, Newport, OR 97365
Web: portofnewport.com/recreational-marina
Phone: 541-867-3321
Watch the Episode: traveloregon.com/WinterCrab

ODFW Crab Class

When you try something new, it pays to go with the pros! Not so long ago, more than thirty newcomers—mostly parents and their kids—discovered how to catch Oregon's premier crustacean: Dungeness crab. The gathering of parents and their kids attended one of the Oregon Department of Fish and Wildlife's (ODFW) Crab Classes, a hands-on seminar from the agency's menu of adventures called Outdoor Skills (dfw.state.or.us/education/outdoor _skills). Instructors, biologists, and volunteers teach and assist students in the varied Outdoor Skills courses.

Crabbing is a popular recreation that requires some skill and knowledge, so the agency developed the daylong course to encourage participation. ODFW spokesperson and instructor Mark Newell said that the students get all the gear and assistance that they might need for a day of fun and excitement at any number of the seminars that are held in various coastal towns including Gold Beach, Bandon, Port Orford, Charleston, and Yaquina Bay at Newport. "We want people to care about the environment and the only way to get them to do that is to get them out enjoying it. That's what Crab Class does for many students," said Newell.

Mike Hoge and his son, Jerrad Hoge, came all the way from Silverton to pick up pointers on the crabbing recreation. "I did it a little bit as a kid," noted Mike. "But I didn't really have any instruction, so I thought some good lessons would help and I'm glad we came today." The students kicked off the affair at the South Beach State Park Activity Center, just south of Newport. Instructor Brandon Ford presented the basics of crab biology and explained the trapping techniques and the rules and regulations of the sport.

The session was followed by a short drive to Yaquina Bay Marina where the hands-on action began. The first order of business was learning how to place the bait inside the crab trap or rings. The bait of choice for the day's adventure: chicken! Jennifer Erickson said that she didn't mind the tradeoff of chicken for crab. In fact, she and her husband, Steve Erickson, traveled from Portland for the chance to learn something new about a seafood they really enjoy eating for dinner. "It's really fun to go out with experts," she noted. "To be coached and helped along the way before doing it on our own just seemed to make a lot of sense to us. Plus, crab is so tasty—that's a bonus."

Once the students were comfortable with the gear, it was time to toss the traps from atop Yaquina Bay Pier that juts hundreds of yards into the bay. The pier is open to fishing and crabbing year-round. Students learned how to measure a crab to make certain it's legal (only twelve male Dungeness crabs are allowed and they must be 5¾ inches across the back) and how to tell the difference between the two species of crab that are present in Yaquina Bay: Dungeness crabs and red rock crabs. "We show them how to crab from the pier," said Ford. "But we also take them out on the bay in boats to drop traps in several places that our biologists have scouted. We try to take folks to the best places in the whole bay."

The traps were checked, the crabs were counted, and then it was time to cook. It was a fine way to round out the day's adventure. Each student in the class must purchase an ODFW Shellfish License. The course costs $40 for adults, $10 for kids under 18. Students are provided with instruction plus all the gear including bait, traps, and life jackets. "It's a real good deal," added Ford. "Especially at lunchtime because no one goes away hungry from the class."

In addition to ODFW's classes, crab seminars are also a part of the annual outdoor celebrations at the Pacific Northwest Sportsman's Show—a 5-day event held each February at the Portland Expo Center—and the annual PDX KidFest and the ODFW's popular Portland Women's Expo.

4

Wahclella Falls and Memaloose Hills

The Columbia River Gorge offers moments of magic through scenic beauty and adventure that come from poking around seldom-seen sites prized for springtime splendor. Wahclella Falls and Memaloose Hills are two of my favorite wildflower and waterfall hikes in the Gorge that are off the beaten path where the dirt takes over.

I call the mile-long trail to Wahclella Falls a "back-pocket hike" because it's handy and easy to reach and just a stone's throw from Bonneville Dam at Columbia River Mile 146. The drama of the falls makes this trail a great choice for hiking with your children (there is even a portable toilet at the trailhead year-round), but be mindful of occasional drop-offs in parts of the canyon. With small children, stay on the lower trail to avoid the sheer-sided return loop near the falls. You'll also traverse bridges and climb some stairs on this hike. Tanner Creek lures you along the gentle trail that has about 300 feet of elevation gain. Watch for foamy sheets of water that drain across canyon rock walls—they are a delight to stop and enjoy before Wahclella Falls explodes into view with deafening style.

Named for an ancient Chinook Indian village site, Wahclella Falls does so in two tiers, dropping 50 and 80 feet respectively out of a narrow gorge. It pours into a large pool at the head of a massive basalt amphitheater and it's an inviting place to enjoy a picnic while the rushing water washes your stress away.

While it is a fine setting for escaping from your daily routine, don't get too comfy for the Gorge has more springtime "wonder falls" to explore—in fact, more than forty of them—and according to famed Oregon landscape photographer Steve Terrill, here's the best part: "They are all so different; Shepperd's Dell Falls

Memaloose Overlook provides a moment of rest and contemplation of so much beauty in the Columbia River Gorge.

sits in a fine little pocket just off the scenic highway, Latourel Falls can be seen right from the roadway, and then Wahkeena Falls sweeps and terraces down all those rocks. Plus, there are so many hiking trails up here that if you want to get away from it all, the Gorge can help you do that."

Near Mosier, discover another excursion with your children that's well off the beaten path when you stroll the Memaloose Hills on a wildflower hike that can take you up to 6 miles and 800 feet in elevation. The trail is jam-packed with flowers including stunning balsamroot, Columbia desert parsley, glacier lily, prairie star, and shooting star. "The Memaloose Hills have become one of Georgjean (Terrill's wife) and my favorite places to enjoy nature's wonderful wildflower shows," said a smiling Steve Terrill on a recent spring day. A day where brilliant sunlight illuminated Gorge scenery that was perfectly suited to add to his stunning Oregon calendars. He added, "The hiking trails are user-friendly, never too crowded, and the variety of flowers almost endless."

Memaloose Hills has two trailheads, one at a scenic overlook pullout on the Historic Columbia River Highway and one at a rest area. When hiking with children, the rest area may be preferable because of the access to a water fountain and restrooms. Memaloose Rest Area is off the eastbound lane of I-84, just 3 miles east of Mosier, Oregon. Walk to the west end of the parking area and watch for the maintenance road. Walk around the sign that says, "No Admittance, Authorized Personnel Only." All this trail is on public land but be advised that there are no trail signs. Follow the trail as it works its way from the rest stop up the hill. Shade soon turns to golden patches of arrowleaf balsamroot punctuated by blue lupine and paintbrush wildflowers. For me, this is an out-and-back hike—returning downhill the same way I walked up.

This public landscape is open anytime thanks to the efforts of a true Columbia Gorge "patriot," Nancy Russell, who founded Friends of the Columbia Gorge in 1980. According to the Friends Executive Director Kevin Gorman, Russell was the reason the Memaloose Hills are now yours to explore as a part of the Columbia River Gorge National Scenic Area. "Nancy would do anything to protect the Gorge, just like a mother would protect her children. She was fierce and protective and she cared quite a bit about this area. She really was a big advocate of the public's right to enjoy special places like this."

The nearly 5,000 acres of the broad Rowena Plateau landscape is just getting started in early April; the peak of the wildflower bloom is still weeks away. "It really is a stunner," added Terrill. "It is probably the most dramatic wildflower display in the Gorge. It is a gorgeous place to look at with the bright and beautiful patches of balsamroot and the brilliant red paintbrush right next to them . . . just an explosion of color up here."

You need to watch where you are stepping in this area for two good reasons. The first is to be sure that you don't sprain an ankle by stepping on one of the football-sized pieces of basalt rock that litter the ground. They are reminders of the Missoula Floods that happened at the end of the last ice age, about 13,000 years ago. And the second reason: poison oak abounds, so take care.

4A Wahclella Falls (Trail #436)

Where: I-84 to exit #40, Bonneville Fish Hatchery. Turn south and follow road to trailhead.

Web: fs.usda.gov

Phone: 541-308-1727

4B Memaloose Hills

Where: For the Rest Area Trailhead: Head east on I-84. Past exit #69 look for milepost 72; 0.8 miles beyond that milpost exit I-84 at the blue Rest Area sign.

Watch the Episode: traveloregon.com/GorgeWildflowers

Hiking with Kids

As with any outdoor adventure when you add kids to the mix, the success of your trip can be improved with a little preparation. Considering the what-ifs before you go will help you be prepared for most any emergency.

First, know your kids. Plan conservatively and expect they may get tired. What do they enjoy and how can you incorporate that into your hike? Perhaps a treasure hunt like geocaching or letterboxing will get them excited about a hike. Or discovering wild animals in their natural habitat. Or the reward of a beautiful vista, cave, waterfall, or lake. Pack a picnic and some games. Use the natural environment to challenge their observation skills (e.g. find something that begins with each letter of the alphabet). Bring binoculars or a magnifying glass. Have the kids make a simple water scope at home (cut the end off a can or carton to make a tube and cover one end with clear plastic); bring it along to explore a river or stream. Your own enthusiasm will go a long way toward making this a fun experience for the whole family.

For any day hike, even if you don't expect to be gone long, prepare as if you had to spend one night in the open. Essentials include a small first aid kit, a whistle for each child, bug spray, sunscreen, healthy snacks, and water. Pack along small, lightweight gear that can serve multiple purposes in a pinch like a synthetic, waterproof jacket or poncho, a thin foil emergency blanket, dry socks, and a pocketknife. Even a small packet of duct tape, paper towels, wet wipes, a plastic bag, and a couple rubber bands can be fashioned in a variety of ways to fix or bandage almost anything.

We sometimes overlook good walking shoes for kids (please, no flip-flops!), but this can make the difference between a happy hike and, well, miles of whining. As Oregonians, it's always a good idea to prepare for rain and dress in layers. It's also useful to keep a garbage bag handy in the car so if legs and shoes get muddy, your kids can just step into the bag for the car ride home.

Take advantage of teachable moments while hiking. Remind your kids to stay on designated trails to protect surrounding plants and habitats. Help them understand the fragility of the ecosystems around them. Pack it in—pack it out.

So take a deep breath, be flexible, see the hike from your child's perspective, and have a great time!

May

5

Forests for Families

O ne of the most intriguing and exciting stories was born in the forest just off
Portland's front step—the Tillamook State Forest. That's where four successive and devastating fires—collectively called the Tillamook Burn—destroyed over 400,000 acres of ancient forest in the last century. The Tillamook Forest Center is located just off Oregon State Highway 6 that links Portland to Tillamook.

The center tells the story of how four devastating fires in the 1930s, '40s, and '50s claimed hundreds of thousands of acres of old-growth forest and how thousands of men battled the flames to protect what they could and then how an army of volunteers brought the forest back to life. Chris Friend, a retired education specialist, said the place is well suited to families who are eager to learn more: "We teach about the pioneers who settled here, the Native Americans who were here for thousands of years, and we tell the stories of the fires and the forest replantings that followed." Ongoing interactive exhibits and interpretive programs are suitable for children of all ages, and special events scheduled throughout the year will keep you coming back for more.

When you're ready, you can leave the center's main exhibit hall to cross the 250-foot-long Wilson River Suspension Bridge or climb up into the clouds—seventy-two steps up—to the top (40 feet high) of a replica fire lookout tower that is adjacent to the center. Back in the 1950s fire lookout towers were common. In fact, fifteen of them dotted the high country in Oregon's North Coast Range.

Lisa Gibson, an education specialist with the Oregon Department of Forestry, said that the replica four-story fire lookout tower provides visitors with

Guided tours at Magness Tree Farm will teach your kids much about the outdoors.

a "snapshot of life" from an earlier era right after WWII. I joined her for the trek to the top of the tower and she said, "It's a beautiful coincidence that there are seventy-two steps to the top because there are 72 million trees planted across the Tillamook State Forest."

Gibson said the women who "manned" fifteen towers atop the remote and rugged Oregon Coast Range Mountains began after WWII and continued through the early 1990s and they were called the Cloud Girls. "It was a really romantic idea," added Gibson. "These young women out by themselves in the forest—living on their own and watching for fire among the clouds and the tops of the trees. People had a vision that included a somewhat romantic image for their service."

They were a special breed of Oregon Department of Forestry personnel because women like Eleanor Mitchell answered a call that few men dared in the late 1940s. Mitchell was prized and admired by all for her patience and willingness to endure lonely weeks in the woods to provide service to the community. "By all accounts, she really enjoyed the job. It was a very important civic responsibility that you had as a fire lookout," added Gibson. "The fire lookouts were key in providing information to field offices to get fire crews ready to attack that fire before it got so big they couldn't control it anymore."

The Tillamook Forest Center is fully accessible inside and has ADA-accessible outdoor trails as well. Baby changing stations and ample picnic areas make this a pleasant destination for the whole family. It is free to visit and filled with educational possibilities.

It's seventy-two steps to the top of the Tillamook Forest Center's four-story-tall fire lookout tower.

As the suburbs grow larger and our pace of life goes faster, it's good to know that some Oregon places provide an outdoor escape into a bit of the backwoods. If you follow Bill Wood's lead, there's a good chance you'll learn something new too.

Wood is a retired "guide" who for years was the man in charge at the Magness Tree Farm. He taught thousands of youngsters much about life in his forest. Magness Tree Farm is an 80-acre parcel tucked into the hills just a handful of miles between Wilsonville and Sherwood, Oregon. The site boasts more than 2 miles of trail; most of it is a fairly gentle grade and as you hike, you will often have Corral Creek by your side.

Down close to ground, take note of the varied wildflowers—a show that begins in April when white-faced trilliums light up the scene. "Most of the spring flowers begin to show in April," noted Wood. "By May, we'll have all kinds of color here that lasts the next 4 or 5 weeks."

Magness is just part of the outdoor education story because it is owned by the nearby World Forestry Center, located in Portland's West Hills adjacent to the Oregon Zoo.

Back in the forest at the Magness Tree Farm, be sure to check out the three rustic cabins that you can rent for a longer stay. Each cabin sleeps up to 12 people and offers electricity, but no heat—so if you spend the night, you want to prepare for colder nights. Reservations are required. Wood said that once folks discover the Magness landscape, they seldom want to leave: "When they first come here, they are awe-inspired by the creek and the serenity of the surroundings. They hear the birds, see the squirrels, and relax with their kids. When we see them a second time, they usually bring another family and so our circle expands. It's really a wonderful place to be and yet you don't have to travel far to get here."

The farm is open daily to the public from dawn to dusk with occasional closures for special events. Easy to moderate trails are well-suited for all ages; there is a ½-mile paved trail with interpretive signs for a self-guided tour to help you see how the forest grows and changes. You can even bring your dog on a leash to hike with you. A small stream, sheltered picnic area, recreation field, and restrooms make this a great place to spend a day in the woods with your family.

5A Tillamook Forest Center

Where: 45500 Wilson River Highway, Tillamook, OR 97141
Web: tillamookforestcenter.org
Phone: 503-815-6800; 866-930-4646
Watch the Episode: traveloregon.com/TillamookForest

5B Magness Tree Farm

Where: 31195 SW Ladd Road, Sherwood, OR 97140
Web: worldforestry.org
Phone: 503-228-1367
Watch the Episode: traveloregon.com/treefarm

6

Written in the Rocks

Who doesn't love a good mystery? I found one near Newport on the Oregon coast.

It's a mystery about the formation of the Oregon coastline and where 12-million-year-old history is written in the rocks. Anyone can crack this case—all you need is a little time and a spirit of adventure.

South Beach State Park, a mile south of Newport, is a jewel in the rough across the Oregon outdoors. The 500-acre parkland offers spacious campgrounds—with nearly 280 sites—that are perfect for tents or trailers. Plus, another thirty yurts for folks who like to camp but lack all the gear. Many of the park's facilities are ADA accessible and throughout the summer months bike rentals are available as well as daily interpretive programs, guided hikes, and Junior Ranger activities. Restrooms and hot showers make the park especially family friendly. Park Ranger Dani Padilla said that South Beach State Park is often coined a "destination vacation" for the varied activities that are easy to find along the central coast. For example, she suggested a guided paddle trip (they are offered 5 days a week) on nearby Beaver Creek: "Paddling on Beaver Creek is one of the most peaceful and one of the closest times you can get in tune with nature. We don't have tidal influence on Beaver Creek so you're not worried about the tides or the waves, and you will see all the migratory birds, eagles, and ospreys." Also nearby the campground are a playground, horseshoe pits, and a 9-hole disc golf course. You can check out horseshoes and discs or pick up maps, brochures, souvenirs, and camp items at the hospitality center.

More than 3 million visitors flock to the 24-mile stretch of beach between

South Newport and Yachats each year. And yet—according to Assistant Park Manager Alan Freudenthal, the search for peace, quiet, and solitude takes very little effort: "You may look a little bit more and you may need to get a little further away from the cities, but places like Brian Booth State Park includes Beaver Creek, Ona Beach, and more—there are great hiking trails throughout that allow you to hike to the top of a mountain and see the ocean and not hear any road noise or see very few people."

You can discover Oregon history that's written in the rocks like this cockle clam fossil that's 12 million years old.

Park Ranger Christopher Maitlen said that beachside agate collecting is a popular recreation, especially with the kids and pays off with gorgeous stones that park visitors can keep. Maitlen is a big fan of the park's interpretive program called Beach Booty 101 and that's no surprise—he's the teacher. The two of us met at Ona Beach and watched the kids frolic in the sand and the knee-deep water—some youngsters were bent over to carefully scan the sand. It was an obvious clue that the kids were looking for treasures. "This is called a *wrack* line, Grant, the line of debris left on the beach by high tide," explained the longtime ranger. "We actually have two wrack lines from the two high tides each day. As you can see, we have a few specimens of agates and shells along this line mixed in with all the vegetation."

Collecting agates is for personal use only! You are allowed 1 gallon per day and you must use your own bucket to collect them. Critically, no digging into the sand is allowed; you must pick the agates off the beach. "That's to keep it from going to commercial use," said Maitlen. "This is for private collections so you can have a memory of your visit to the coast." Maitlen loves to share his own collections that show you what you might find for very little effort; not just agates or jaspers but fossils that date back more than 12 million years and where he insisted, "Oregon history is written in the rocks."

"Creatures—mostly clams or snails—are frozen in time, captured in layers of sandstone," he said. "It's kinda funny—there they were, living a happy day on the beach just like you or I might, and then all of a sudden a dramatic explosion occurred and silt and volcanic ash covered them up. Through millions of years, pressure and heat fossilized the shell matter."

Maitlen explained that Oregon was once a tropical landscape with volcanic activity a constant marker of time—tying to understand how it all changed is a part of the mystery that he loves to consider: "The rocks and fossils humble me when I consider the passage of so much time that I can hold right in my hand. I know that I am just a speck on this planet for a fraction of time and Oregon State Parks rangers and other staff feel it's important that we offer visitors the chance to find these treasures too. It's a wonderful thing and we'll continue to offer assistance to families that want to enjoy agate collecting. So get out here and take a walk because the agate beds are where you find them."

Agates are found all along the Oregon coast, but this stretch from South Newport to Yachats can be especially bountiful. Be sure to check the tide schedule and do your beachcombing during outgoing tide to readily access the high-tide wrack lines and uncovered gravel. Venturing out after a storm can yield positive results as stormy waves deposit new finds on the beach. Agates are usually translucent and can be easier to find when still wet and shining in the sun. Also keep an eye out for petrified wood and fossilized shells. If you start your agate hunt at Brian Booth State Park you will find restrooms, picnic tables, and a paved parking area.

6A South Beach State Park

Where: 5044 Oregon Coast Highway, South Beach, OR 97366
Web: oregonstateparks.org
Phone: 800-551-6949; 541-867-7451

6B Brian Booth State Park/Ona Beach

Where: Spans US Highway 101 at the intersection with North Beaver Creek Road, 1.6 miles north of Seal Rock, OR 97376
Web: oregonstateparks.org
Phone: 800-551-6949; 541-867-7451

Watch the Episode: traveloregon.com/RockWriting

On the Coast with the Kids

A trip to the coast can be fun, exciting, and relaxing all in one, but parents need to know the risks. Situations change rapidly at the beach: tides, sneaker waves, sinkholes, and sandbars can create a tricky environment. The best way to ensure your family stays safe is to pay attention and stick together. It's tempting to relax on the sand with a good book while your kids frolic in the surf, but always stay with your children in the water. Regardless of whether they are strong swimmers, waves can quickly upend a child and rip currents can pull strongly even when just wading in the water. Having an adult within arm's reach can prevent disaster.

Keep foremost in your mind the phrase "Never turn your back on the ocean." Oregon's sneaker waves are exactly that—sneaky—and they can catch your whole family off guard. It's easy to lose your balance in the sand when quickly surrounded by these high-washing waves. Or worse, to be toppled off a drift log you thought was well beyond the ocean's reach. Never allow children to play on or around beached logs as just a small film of water can lift them far enough off the sand to roll over children and adults. Even small logs can be waterlogged and far too heavy to lift. And sneaker waves can carry with them a literal ton of sand that can weigh you down quickly.

Cliffs and rocks can be equally dangerous as wave and current patterns vary around these formations. Cliffs can be unstable and rocks can have sharp or rough edges and be slippery at any time. Use caution and never consider these natural features as play areas.

Even in familiar areas, unexpected changes in topography or landmarks can occur. The ocean is ever-changing and the hazards on a particular beach the previous summer may be completely different during a different season or the next year. Before you go, familiarize yourself with riptides, rip currents, and undertows. Know how to spot and avoid them, and educate yourself and your children on what to do if you encounter them. Swim parallel to shore until you escape a current's path. Always obey posted warnings and off-limits areas.

A trip to the coast is a wonderful way to build lasting memories with the whole family. Remaining vigilant during your visit helps ensure those memories are all positive.

7

King of the Clam Gun

As springtime moves into high gear, the best low tides of the season bring a bounty of seafood close at hand. Oregon's beaches are popular year-round destinations for many reasons, but in Clatsop County there's a famous sandy stretch at Fort Stevens State Park that turns into "Clam Heaven" for thousands of people who show up to dig their suppers from the sea.

Local resident Steve Fick likes to say, "When the tide goes out, the dinner table is set—with razor clams!" Fick grew up in Astoria and he really *digs* this recreation: "Oh, Grant, there are clams galore this season—one of the best, most plentiful clam 'sets' in recent history. The biologists say the harvest could exceed 1 million clams. Wow, huh?" That much is certain, but if you or the kids have never dug this sport—how do you get started?

Fick handed me a "clam gun," the tool of choice for beginners learning the ropes of clam digging. It was a hard plastic tube, with a covered top that has a handle built into it, plus there is a small hole on the top so that the tube acts like a siphon.

Each razor clam digger is allowed a limit of fifteen clams.

You press the tube or "gun" down into the soft sand up to 3 feet deep, and then place your thumb over the hole, lift, and pull the tube full of sand—and hopefully, the razor clam—back up to the surface. "Try that clam hole right there, Grant," advised Fick. He pointed to a small, quarter-sized

Clam digging is an Oregon family tradition because it's so easy, anyone can dig a limit.

dimple in the sandy surface. "The clam's neck is just under that dimple. It's a give-away sign that there's a clam down there. Go for it!"

And so I did—the tube easily slid down the hole's length, then I covered it and lifted the heavy tube full of sand that held a dandy 4-inch-long razor clam. The entire process was slick, so easy that anyone can do it! In recent years, razor clam digging has only improved. At Bell Buoy of Seaside, a seafood specialty store, Jon Hartill said his workers clean and vacuum-pack more than 800 pounds of razor clams each week during a season stretching from April through July. He added that the hand-work techniques for cleaning and processing the clams hasn't changed in decades. "This is a pretty old, traditional way of doing it—all by hand and nothing fancy here," noted Hartill. "Sixty percent of our clams go to restaurants and they want a consistent size so that's usually eleven or twelve clams to the pound."

Bell Buoy also sells fresh clams to the public as fast as they are placed in the cooler. In fact, the store is the only Oregon processor of fresh razor clams. "I think there is a huge demand for razor clams—especially in Portland," added Hartill. "I think people taste these Oregon clams that are so sweet and tender and that immediately takes them to the beach. It's kind of neat that way."

Each spring, more than 800,000 razor clams are harvested off 18 miles of shoreline between Seaside and the Columbia River. Oregon Department of Fish and Wildlife's Matt Hunter is a shellfish biologist who monitors the size, age, and quality of the daily commercial clam catch. Hunter said that Mother Nature delivered a record amount of razor clams to the Oregon coast in recent years: "We seem to be setting new records of abundance each year! The ocean currents are right and the productivity of the ocean seems better and we get this tremendous set of clams on our beaches. Plus, we've had mild winters in the past ten years and that helps overall clam survival. People will have no problem digging their limits of fifteen razor clams!"

Back on the beach—near the *Peter Iredale* shipwreck at Fort Stevens State Park, Paul Watt said that one man's recreation is actually his "research." "I love coming out here on a minus low tide to dig on the sandbars that are revealed—it's really good clamming when that happens." Watt doesn't mind wading knee-deep through chilly saltwater so he can try out his latest clam gun model that takes the strain out of the sport. You see, Watt designs and builds the popular tools that many folks use to catch their supper from the sea.

"Clam digging is really addicting," said Watt. "You never know if it'll be a big one or a little one—it's just a lot of fun and I love it!" Watt is a structural engineer by education and a welder by trade, but the lifelong "coastie" has earned a nickname over the past 3 decades: "King of the Clam Gun" for the innovative clam guns that he creates.

Inside his welding shop in Bay City, Oregon, he cuts out the parts, shapes the tubes, and attaches the handles, but he doesn't use plastic or aluminum—rather, Watt prefers stainless steel: "The stainless is very thin and yet it's strong enough to stand up to the pushing and pulling through thick sand. Plus, it's really a slick metal so it goes into the sand easier." And if you're a clam digger, "easier" equals more efficient use of your energy as you lift out several pounds of sand with each pull of the clam gun.

Watt has added a new feature to his clam gun that really takes the strain out of the sport. Diggers have long complained that the clam gun's sand vacuum slows them down and leads to sore backs as they struggle to lift the sand-filled guns. So Watt has added a tiny release valve near the bottom of the gun that's made the sport easier than ever: "You're in the water digging and the tiny valve breaks the vacuum that is created when you push the gun down. So when you pull it up, the valve opens and releases the sand vacuum and it's easier to pull."

He's also built a shorter and lighter child's model, so youngsters can easily dig a limit too. And what does Watt like to do with all those daily limits of delicious razor clams: "We broil 'em in the oven. Put a little breading on each and the flavor stays—just 5 minutes or less under the broiler and they are perfect." Watt's recipe is absolutely delicious and provides a fine way to round out the day's adventure. You should know that good clamming tides occur each May and June. If you choose to go, check your tide table and plan your visit at least 2 hours before the low tide.

The Oregon Department of Fish and Wildlife manages the clam resource and there are important rules and regulations to note: a state shellfish license is required for clam diggers 14 and older. Each clam digger must dig their own limit of fifteen razor clams and you *cannot* put any back. Remember: even if you break a shell or dig a small clam, the first fifteen you dig you must keep. Clam map brochures are available at many Oregon Department of Fish and Wildlife offices or you can go to their website and download the maps to take with you when you visit the coast (dfw.state.or.us; search on "clam maps"). You can purchase Paul Watt's clam guns directly from his shop, Watt Welding (9815 9th Street, Bay City, OR; 503-377-2225), and from Englund Marine and Industrial Supply in Astoria.

7A Fort Stevens State Park

Where: 100 Peter Iredale Road, Hammond, OR 97121
Web: oregonstateparks.org
Phone: 503-861-3170 x21; 800-551-6949

7B Bell Buoy of Seaside

Where: 1800 S Roosevelt Drive, Seaside, OR 97138
Web: bellbuoyofseaside.com
Phone: 503-738-2722; 800-529-2722

Watch the Episode: traveloregon.com/DigforDinner

8

Treasures from the Earth— Richardson's Rock Ranch

Armed with rock hammers, shovels, and insatiable appetites for the unexpected, my wife, Chris, and I were anxious to do some digging in the dirt—and it didn't take long to hit pay dirt. The technique isn't too difficult: simply kneel down and hammer, scrape, chisel, and mine the dirt away from the egg. "Rock hounds love to get dirty," declared Casey Richardson. So bring a bucket, gloves, and rock pick (Richardson's provides a bucket and rock hammer for your use) to dig Oregon's treasured state rock from the dirt.

Thundereggs became Oregon's official state rock in 1965 and they are small as marbles but can reach basketball size. "Each one of them is different and if you dig a couple thousand pounds like I have, you go home with quite a feeling of accomplishment. It's a ton o' fun," said the smiling Richardson.

Filling a 5-gallon bucket is no sweat and didn't take us long—then the real fun began back at the rock shop. Richardson's lifetime of experience enabled him to make a slice through one of our eggs at just the right angle with a diamond-embedded saw blade to reveal the rock's interior. Thundereggs were first discovered in this area during the 1920s by a rancher named Leslie Priday. For the past 40 years, the Richardson family has owned and operated its recreational rock ranch for eager tourists who can dig their own treasures or purchase them inside a small lapidary shop.

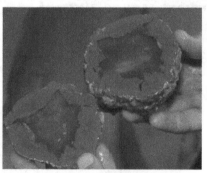

Each thunderegg holds a colorful agate design inside.

Digging thundereggs is so easy anyone—at any age—can find a genuine treasure.

When they are cut open, they reveal agates of various colors and exquisite designs that stand out when they're polished. As we waited for the automated saw blade to slice open all of our prizes, Richardson showed off his most valuable thunderegg called a Priday Plume. He called it "one in a thousand" and it was easy to see what he meant for it looked fabulous with varied hues of blues, greens, and reds. He proudly noted, "It's unique for its size and how clean each plume is. It's a phenomenal piece."

Richardson's displays inside the shop are real showstoppers too with rows of gorgeous thundereggs and other exotic-looking rocks from across the world. You'll discover that thundereggs can be made into beautiful, varied jewelry, especially pendants, pen stands, and bookends. Family photos show off four generations of Richardsons that have kept the business moving forward.

Meanwhile, back in the workshop, Richardson said it's the surprise of it all that continues to excite him. Once a rock is cut open, each provides a lasting memory of time well spent in the Oregon outdoors. As another Richardson family member told me, "The really neat part is that when you dig up a thunderegg and bring it down to have us cut it open, you're the first person to have ever seen that rock. And to think it took 60 million years to make it, plus there's no two alike, they're all different—and the next one is going to be the very prettiest one you've ever cut."

I discovered that the simple beauty and complexity of these geologic wonders are best appreciated when the egg is carefully cracked open and placed on display to reveal a moment from the distant past that's been frozen in time. The sanding and polishing reveal depth and features that are beautiful and unique—just like the state that the rock represents. "Everybody likes to get outdoors as a family and do something together," said Richardson. "Maybe you get a little dirty digging in the ground. But you get to take your prizes home, and a 5-gallon bucket of thundereggs only costs about 50 dollars. That's not bad for a day together." While the shop is open 7 days a week, digging is seasonal and dependent on weather, so be sure to call ahead for availability. Several thunderegg beds provide a range of digging experiences for all ages from easy sorting to hard rock mining. Pets are welcome on a leash, but must remain in the car at the shop.

8A Deschutes River State Recreation Area

Where: 90910 Biggs-Rufus Highway, Wasco, OR 97065
Web: oregonstateparks.org
Phone: 541-739-2322; 800-551-6949

8B Richardson's Rock Ranch

Where: 6683 NE Hay Creek Road, Madras, OR 97741
Web: richardsonrockranch.com
Phone: 541-475-2680; 800-433-2680 (call before 5:00 PM PST)
Watch the Episode: traveloregon.com/ThunderEggs

June

9

Columbia Gorge Sternwheeler

A journey up the Columbia River Gorge is always a treat for me. It's the chance to reconnect with special scenery and places and activities in one of the most beautiful places on the planet. There are so many faces to the Columbia River Gorge: it's a place where light and shadow dance across ancient basalt cliffs that rise hundreds of feet above a river that takes the breath away for its size and power.

It is a place where you can discover vivid scenery that fills the senses as you trek across hiking trails that lead you into new territory. Perhaps your journey allows you to go face-to-face with the most amazing collection of thundering waterfalls in Oregon. There is so much, so close and so easy to reach when you visit.

"Cascade Locks is indeed the heart of the Gorge," noted Cascade Locks resident Holly Howell. "Our community is surrounded by the Columbia Gorge National Scenic Area and that is why our hillside views are so pristine." Howell is also the development manager for the Port of Cascade Locks and said it isn't a matter of finding enough to do in the Gorge, but rather "finding enough time to do it all."

We visited the newest public venue for hikers and bikers called the EasyCLIMB (Cascade Locks International Mountain Biking) Trail on the eastern edge of town. The new 3-mile-loop trail is awash in color right now with brilliant blue camas and

Captain Tom Cramblett allows youngsters to steer the course aboard the sternwheeler Columbia Gorge.

The sternwheeler Columbia Gorge *keeps tradition alive on its daily runs from Cascade Locks.*

chocolate lilies, plus an unmatched view to the Columbia River. We also enjoyed a view to a nesting pair of osprey that are raising their young.

"The trail was built by volunteers who gave more than 1,200 hours of labor to design and build a family-friendly trail to draw people to the sport of mountain biking but it has been embraced by a lot of our locals who enjoy walking their dogs too." The Cascade Locks Marine Park is a spacious public setting for a picnic lunch and also the launching point for 2-hour river trips aboard the sternwheeler *Columbia Gorge*. The park is the location of the historic locks and has a marina, visitor center, children's playground, fifteen designated camping sites with shower building, a community garden, and public restrooms; many of the facilities are ADA accessible. Outdoor PG movie viewings are held several evenings each summer. The park is also home to the local Historical Museum that offers visitors a chance to learn more about the "real" Cascade Locks.

Pat Power is the volunteer caretaker of the small museum that offers interpretive exhibits, artifacts, and a stunning photo collection chronicling the building of the locks. "Before the locks were built," noted Power, "boats from Portland could only come up the Columbia River to an area near the Bonneville Dam area—there they would dock and everything was off-loaded and transported up here to bypass the dangerous Cascade Rapids. From here, they could get onto another sternwheeler and continue further east."

The photo collection captures one of Oregon's most ambitious construction projects of the 1800s. The Cascade Locks were built to ease the river journey around the treacherous Cascade Rapids. The project included over 3,000 feet of canal with three giant steel gates and took more than 20 years to complete.

The Historical Museum was a part of the project too! It was built by the Army Corps of Engineers in 1905. "They built three houses here and they still stand. Each house was aligned with the gates in the lock. The lock masters and their families lived in the homes and they went right out the front door to work each day—just a few yards away," said Power. Just outside the museum, in a small climate-controlled building, you'll find the Oregon Pony steam locomotive on display—the first of its kind to be built and used in the Oregon Territory beginning in 1862.

Back in the park, you'll also notice one of the newest features of the community—an art in the park project that includes three bronze statues by local bronze sculptor Heather Söderberg-Greene. The statues include Sacajawea and the great Newfoundland dog named Seaman. Both were members of the famed Lewis and Clark Expedition that passed this way more than two centuries ago. Cascade Locks is the sort of timeless place that invites you to sit, put your feet up, and watch the river and the world flow by—and it's waiting for you—anytime!

It's also the home port for the sternwheeler *Columbia Gorge*. Folks come from all over to board the ship and Captain Tom makes sure the experience is spectacular. As he likes to say, "It's the most important part of my job!" He added, "There are no propellers, no bow thrusters, so it's all about wind and current. The boat responds the way a paddlewheel boat would have in the 1800s." Captain Tom Cramblett stepped aboard the *Columbia Gorge* in 1982 just after it was built and delivered to Cascade Locks. He worked his way up the ranks to become one of two skippers to guide the sternwheeler on daily tours. He said that sternwheelers arrived on the Columbia River in 1850 at a time when shipping goods and people on the giant waterway was the only practical means of transportation.

When the locks opened in 1896, they offered easy passage for steamboats delivering food, supplies, and people through the Gorge. Cramblett explained, "The area doesn't grow without it! The ships moved all the farming goods, moved all the people, and if you were going to get somewhere in the Columbia River basin, it was the paddleboat that got you there."

These days, the *Columbia Gorge* is all about recreation as passengers enjoy unique sights and sounds, including bald eagles, osprey—even peregrine falcons.

Cramblett said he is always on the lookout for ways to "wow" his passengers no matter their age. He invited young Cameron Norton to climb aboard the captain's chair and help steer the ship. The 4-year-old eagerly followed the captain's orders and sported a big smile while he steered a straight course. The youngster's dad, Jeremy Norton, stood a few feet away and said, "I used to go on this when I was a kid, so to bring my own son out here is fantastic!" The *Columbia Gorge* sternwheeler is operated by Portland Spirit. It operates daily from May through October and offers brunch and dinner cruises, 1- to 2-hour narrated Gorge sightseeing cruises, and a longer Gorge landmarks cruise. Children are welcome and snacks and restrooms are available onboard. Note that the sternwheeler docks in Portland during winter months for maintenance.

---

9 Port of Cascade Locks Marine Park/Historical Museum

Where: 427 Portage Road, Cascade Locks, OR 97014

Web: portofcascadelocks.org

Phone: 541-374-8619

Watch the Episode: traveloregon.com/cascadelocks

Columbia Gorge Sternwheeler

Where: Cascade Locks Marine Park, 299 Portage Road, Cascade Locks, OR 97014

Web: portlandspirit.com/sternwheeler.php

Phone: 503-224-3900

Watch the Episode: traveloregon.com/Steernwheeler

10

Oregon Railriders

The people of Elgin, Oregon, take pride in their railroading heritage and will make you and the family feel right at home when you visit the Elgin Depot and step aboard the Eagle Cap Excursion Train. Dave Arnold is the engineer at the controls of the GP7 diesel electric and he loves to brag: "I get the best seat in the house and I just love the view too." Arnold said the train's engine produces 1,500 horsepower and travels on the historic Joseph Branch Line that was built in 1884. "It is never the same trip," noted the longtime railroad engineer. "I think rolling along on a historic line that's still intact is exciting."

The Eagle Cap Excursion Train is a one-of-a-kind rail trip where the Wallowa or Grande Ronde Rivers are always by your side. It's also a railroad saved from ruin by local folks who believed there was value in holding on to their heritage—so they bought the railroad line in 2003. Stephen Adams, a member of the Wallowa-Union County Railroad Authority, said that the scenic qualities are only a part of the railroad's appeal: "This is the only line in the country where a substantial amount of the track is in roadless terrain. That means this railroad is the only means for visitors to really explore this country—and we love visitors."

It turns out that 63 miles up the same railroad line, another group has given new life to an old, out-of-use rail section. But you won't find a diesel electric engine here—instead, it's a helmet for your head (you can bring your own bike helmet if you'd like), a seat belt to keep you safe, and pedals you have to push when you join in the fun of the Joseph Branch Railriders. The unique car has four wheels that ride the rails and two recumbent adjustable seats than can accommodate riders up to 285 pounds. Young children who cannot reach the pedals (generally age 4 and younger) can ride with an adult, with their car seat strapped into the adjacent rail-rider seat. Infants younger than 6 months may ride in a chest carrier. Each car has a basket for your small belongings and two cup holders per seat. Kim Metlen—a former cycling store owner, designed the cars—or are they bikes?—5 years ago. In 2012, he launched a business that shows off the countryside on a 12-mile stretch from Joseph to Enterprise. "You are gliding down the track; there's no resistance and it's awesome. You don't have to steer, just peddle, so everybody's looking around at the mountains, and the wildlife. The riders all get the same silly little grin and it's worth coming back for the silly little grin."

Metlen added that the business has really taken off—4,000 passengers his third summer, four times the previous year's traffic. "A third of those visitors told me that this activity brought them to Wallowa County for the first time and that they will be back. We are making a difference to the local economy." Making reservations online is recommended; check the company's policies for cancellations and refunds.

Once you reach Enterprise, it's turnaround time and that's an easy effort because the all-aluminum frame and axles and polyurethane wheels weigh a mere 100 pounds. The return trip requires more peddling effort due to the 1½ percent

There's no steering aboard a railrider so you simply peddle and enjoy the scenery.

grade, but the scenery is so pleasing you hardly notice and the trip speeds by. The towering Wallowa Mountains provide a stunning feature that's always by your side. This most family-friendly outing is 12 miles round-trip and takes approximately 2 hours (there is a restroom at the turnaround point). A more challenging excursion is their 6-hour, 26-mile round-trip adventure from Minam to Wallowa. In either case, it is the sort of ride that puts a smile on your face and the sort of setting that keeps it there all day.

10A Elgin Depot

Where: 300 N. 8th Street, Elgin, OR 97827
Web: eaglecaptrainrides.com
Phone: 800-323-7330 (Alegre Travel for reservations)

10B Joseph Branch Railriders

Where: 304 North Main Street, Joseph, OR 97846
Web: jbrailriders.com
Phone: 541-910-0089

Watch the Episode: traveloregon.com/JosephRiders

11

The Lake Born of Fire

When the mood to move strikes each spring, there are few places I like to be more than Oregon's high Cascade Mountains and there are few ways that I prefer to travel more than taking my home on the road in an RV. Recently, my wife, Chris, and I packed up a rental RV from our good friends at RV Northwest in Tigard, Oregon. We traveled to a place that I remember visiting as a child and I was eager to see Clear Lake once again!

Clear Lake is nicknamed the "lake born of fire." It formed over 3,000 years ago when a lava eruption reached the McKenzie River and backed up water to form Clear Lake. The waters are so clear, it is hard to see where the water ends and the bottom of the lake begins. This is the place many of my fishing and camping adventures began as a child—and the same can be said for my three sons as well! It is simply delightful to visit whenever the mood strikes because the lake and the campground-resort areas are open year-round.

Early recreation arrived at Clear Lake in the late 1920s when the Santiam Fish and Game Association (SFGA) was formed by nearby Linn County residents who wanted to protect the lake. "There were businessmen, doctors, lawyers, you name it," said longtime SFGA member Dale Wollam. "They were work-

Many youngsters catch their first trout at Clear Lake.

ing men and for anyone who had a liking for the outdoors, this was just a pretty place to come visit."

The CCC (Civilian Conservation Corps) built the campground in the 1930s—in fact, a group shelter still stands from those early days and you can see the rough-hewn logs and name markers identifying its construction date and the CCC crew who built it. SFGA member Bud Barnes added, "I think most people came up here and stayed several days because we kept the prices down to the point where a working man could come here and afford to stay for a week without completely breaking him."

The SFGA built cabins, a store, docks, and rental boats—and the place thrived year-round as an *affordable* getaway, according to Wollam. "It's been a great destination spot for so many decades. People can come up and enjoy the history of this country. You can camp or stay in a rustic cabin that was built back in the 1920s or a more modern, ADA-accessible cabin with hot running water and a toilet and shower. The best part for many is that there are no streetlights to interrupt things— if you want to go out and look at the stars, you can actually see 'em." Restaurant, grocery store, and service station resources are located in Belknap Springs, about 22 miles from Clear Lake Resort.

I wondered about Barnes's favorite memories throughout more than 5 decades of membership. He offered that it was the "camaraderie and friendship" of the work parties that he enjoyed the most: "Each spring and fall we had what we called a work party—we closed the lodge for a couple of days and we'd get about 50 volunteers to come up here. They'd go around and winterize the place, drain all the pipes, button it all up for winter, and everybody would bring something to share at an evening meal. Boy, it was some of the best meals any of us ever saw."

The SFGA membership peaked in the 1980s with more than 800 members, but by 2007, the group numbered 200. Barnes said that membership dwindled because families were pulled in so many different directions and the idea of getting away from it all languished. In 2007, Linn County bought the site and manages it in partnership with the US Forest Service.

Despite the changing of the guard and the changing of the times, family traditions continue today at Clear Lake—more often than not, with a rod, reel, and bucket of night crawlers. Visitors like Lebanon resident Will Tucker, who brought his granddaughter 11-year-old Stella Lang with him, were having a ball on the lake catching rainbow trout. "We always catch at least one," noted Tucker. "So we can have a trout for dinner. Stella has caught a nice one today that's little more than 14 inches long. To date, all of my children caught their first fish on this lake and

Many youngsters catch their first trout at Clear Lake.

six of my grandchildren have caught their first fish here. Clear Lake is a mecca for trout fishing folks—even better, it's open year-round."

Tucker grew up playing at Clear Lake as a kid and he loves to share its beauty—and its secrets, like the easy hike (along a looped trail around the lake) to reach the underground spring that feeds Clear Lake. We followed his lead until we arrived at a crystal clear pool—so clear you could see every rock and piece of wood on the bottom. Tucker said the clarity is very deceiving. "As you see, the springs look like 20 or 30 feet deep but it's not! It's 50 to 60 feet deep and so cold—36 degrees—so you can't swim to the bottom. The water is the purest you're ever going to find! It's been filtered by miles and miles of lava from Cascade Mountains like Mt. Washington and Mt. Jefferson."

The Clear Lake Loop is a nearly 6-mile offshoot of the McKenzie River Trail that circles Clear Lake and passes the headwaters of the McKenzie River. It's open to hikers and mountain bikers, but the west side of the trail closes periodically to protect nesting bald eagles. The back side of the loop can be challenging for novice bike riders as it weaves through lava fields, so children may need to walk their bike through the difficult areas. Check with the ranger at Clear Lake before you set out on your hike. The popular trail is rated as moderate in difficulty and is usually open from late spring until the first snow of fall.

Tucker also showed me many of the lake's submerged trees, part of a forest that's as old as the lake: "These trees that you see underwater, they were captured or trapped by the lava flow that created the lake—they were submerged when the water backed up. They still stand in the lake because the water is so cold—too cold to rot and they've been here 3,000 years. There are dozens and dozens of these and it will be thousands of years before they disappear. These trees would have been a forest just like the one we are looking at surrounding the lake today—until Mother Nature turned it into a lake. It's a pretty incredible place to visit." The resort focuses on quiet family activities so no motorboats are allowed. Instead, you can plan to spend your time fishing in rowboats or canoes, hiking, biking, and wildlife watching. While the cold water generally makes the lake unsuitable for swimming, scuba divers enjoy discovering the lake's sunken forest and lava flows. Clear Lake is all of that and even more. The sort of place that lets you set your clock back, relax, and enjoy—it's Oregon!

---

11 Clear Lake Resort

Where: NF-775, Sisters, OR 97413, located on Highway 126, 4 miles south
    of the Highway 20 junction
Web: linnparks.com/parks/clear-lake-resort
Phone: 541-967-3917

A Word About Children and Safety on the Water

Accidents on the water happen too fast to put on a life jacket in an emergency. US Coast Guard statistics show that drowning was the reported cause of death in almost three-fourths of recreational boating fatalities in 2015, and that 84 percent of those who drowned were not wearing life jackets. That's why boating safety advocates continue to push for increased and consistent life jacket wear on the water.

Remember: Children age 12 and under must wear a US Coast Guard approved life jacket at all times while on an open deck or cockpit of vessels that are underway or when being towed. Inflatable personal flotation devices (PFDs) are not approved for children under 16. All boats must carry at least one US Coast Guard approved PFD/life jacket for every person aboard. Persons being towed are considered onboard. PFDs must be in serviceable condition. They must not have any rips, tears, or broken straps. All life jackets must also be kept "readily accessible" for use in an emergency. Life jackets in a plastic bag or in a storage compartment are not readily accessible.

Life jacket designs are much more comfortable, lightweight, and stylish than the old, bulky orange style most boaters envision. Life jackets that use inflatable technologies keep the wearer cool and comfortable and resemble a pair of suspenders or a belt pack. Many inflate automatically when immersed in water. Other life jacket styles are available for almost any boating activity:

- **For fishing:** Vest-style life jackets come with features such as pockets and clips to replace the traditional fishing vest and keep the angler safe.

*It's Oregon law - all kids, 12 years and younger,
must wear a properly fitting life jacket.*

- **For children:** Virtually all styles are available sized especially for children —some with cartoon characters, straps for pulling children from the water, and high-visibility schemes.

No matter what the activity or style chosen, the most important thing is this: remember to grab a life jacket and "Wear It!" —*Courtesy of the Oregon State Marine Board*

12

Campsite with a View— Timothy Lake

When my sons were mere youngsters, there was a popular shout-out that I made to them each year as soon as school let out: "Who wants to go camping?" I roared, always trying my best to suppress a sly grin on those sun-blessed June mornings. Perhaps a half second passed before an ecstatic chorus erupted from my three young boys standing nearby. They chimed in at once:

"Me, me, me!"

"Yeah, yeah, yeah!"

"I do, I do, I do!"

Overjoyed that vacation time had finally arrived, my sons' anticipation was at an all-time high. By then I had been building the suspense for weeks about just where we might make our first-of-the-season spring campout. Now everyone wanted to know where we were going. Fact is, we McOmies are not ones to let the grass grow under our feet; we're a family on the move when the warm season strikes, bound for new adventures, places to see, people to meet, and activities to enjoy as we build memories of family time together.

I am a big believer that some of the best adventures can be found right in our own backyards, so we were on the fast track into the Mt. Hood National Forest, a little less than 2 hours from Portland, to enjoy a quiet midweek break at a most delightful lake in the forest. Timothy Lake is certainly close to the Portland metropolitan area, yet it remains a distant world away from urban pavement and noise.

We headed into the Cascades on US 26 and veered right at the junction just past Government Camp with Skyline Road (also known as Forest Service Road 42), which zips through woods with nary a house or meadow to be seen. Skyline

Road, paved all the way to Oakridge, is a major artery for recreation travel and is one of many Forest Service roads that lace the Oregon Cascades. Before long, we arrived at the 1,500-acre lake that offers four campgrounds: Gone Creek, Oak Fork, Pine Point, and—our favorite—Hoodview. Collectively, these campgrounds provide more than 200 campsites and several picnic areas along the lakeshore.

Timothy Lake is really a reservoir that was formed in 1956 when Portland General Electric dammed the Oak Fork of the Clackamas River for electric power generation. According to US Forest Service District Ranger Kathleen Walker, the entire area was once the historic site of Timothy Meadows, which had been a favorite area for summer grazing of sheep. Walker told me that sheepherders spread Timothy grass to enrich the native grasses that grew on the meadows, hence the name Timothy Lake. The circular lake rests behind a 110-foot-high, 740-foot-long dam and is primarily popular for its camping and fishing opportunities. In fact, on this early June adventure I had arranged to connect with my longtime fishing partner, Trey Carskadon, who enjoys exploring all the Cascade watery nooks and crannies that hold hungry trout. He's made a summer pilgrimage to Timothy Lake ever since he was a young boy, and he was anxious to show us around the lake.

Once our family trailer had been set on its camping site at Hoodview—with a spectacular overlook of the lake and surrounding forest—we couldn't get tackle boxes, rods, reels, and bait unpacked fast enough. After all, I had three eager anglers leading the charge, and it was all I could do to grab a cooler full of lunch, rein in the boys, then race ahead fast enough to prevent a McOmie stampede onto Trey's 22-foot fishing boat. He had been standing by, his boat warmed and ready to troll all of us across the lake. He said he had just the ticket to help us catch our dinner. But as I stepped aboard, I noticed how quickly the weather had changed from stunning sunshine disappearing and playing peekaboo as milky white wisps washed in from the west to skirt the top of the forest.

A light breeze carried a late afternoon chill that joined our fishing adventure.

"Mighty cold weather for June, my friend," I remarked as I shivered and Trey set the boat's course to parallel the lake's shoreline.

"Yes, yes, it is." With a chuckle he added, "And this is the banana belt of the Cascades. We're only at 3,000 feet in elevation! But at this time of year the weather can change in a heartbeat, so you have to be prepared with warm clothing. Now the upside is that the fish are definitely biting. In fact, today it's been red-hot!"

That's exactly what I was hoping to hear, and it whet my appetite as we joined Trey and his partner Eric Aronson. They were using lightweight fishing rods, reels, and small spinners called "rooster tails," which are available in a variety of colors.

(Trey prefers brown, black, and green.) As an added bonus to attract the trout, Trey placed a small night crawler on each lure's hooks. He called it a bit of extra insurance that almost always guarantees a bite.

Timothy Lake is a favorite recreational site, particularly for Portland-area residents, because tens of thousands of rainbow trout are stocked annually by the Oregon Department of Fish and Wildlife. You may also catch brook trout, cutthroat trout, or kokanee (a smallish, landlocked sockeye salmon) from the lake's cold waters. Within moments, my young Eric, always anxious to catch a fish, had a silvery 14-inch rainbow trout hooked, splashing, and ready to net. As I admired the darting flashes reflected from the fat and sassy trout, I also noticed the telltale crimson marks along its deep-bodied sides. I asked Trey about the rainbow trout stocking program at Timothy.

"That's really a nice trout, Trey, and you say this size is typical of Timothy trout?"

"That's correct, Grant. The Oregon Fish and Wildlife Department does a great job keeping this lake stocked with trout all summer long. Thousands will be planted, and interestingly, anglers will catch most of the fish by season's end in September. People come from all over the Northwest to fish this lake. And by the way, Grant—you've got one on!"

Yikes! I did—a gorgeous trout easily pushing the tape at 14 inches or more. And with that, as though some god of the trout bite had pushed a "fish on" button, each of us in turn grabbed our rods that had been bent into horseshoe-shaped pretzel affairs by the strong diving pulls of the fighting fish. Fins and tails were splashing, as the trout went dashing while the kids were laughing—and all of it was marvelous! We were in the midst of a trout feeding frenzy, and we were the special guests. Trey really knew the lake and the trout and offered some advice for the novice visitor.

"Probably the best tip that I can give," he said, "and it applies to any of the high Cascade lakes in the Mt. Hood National Forest, is to pay attention to what other people around you are doing. It may seem obvious, but watch to see what the successful anglers are using to catch trout. Also, too many people who are new to these lakes say, 'Well, it's deeper out there in the middle of the lake, so that must be where more fish live.' Not true! My experience has been, especially early in the season, just the opposite. Today, we're only trolling 20 yards from shore in 20 to 30 feet of water. That's because the water's warmer here from the radiant sun. And it's where the fish are feeding. So stick close to shore and you'll catch more."

Within a couple of hours, our limits were filled and we'd arrived back at camp for a shore-side supper of grilled trout. Then we enjoyed the crackling warmth of a campfire, as my wife, Christine, passed cups of steaming hot cocoa all around. We told fish stories, exchanged jokes, and spooky stories that left our sides sore from the giggling and laughing, and soaked up the scenery of a fading sunset that shone across a dazzling Mt. Hood. I raised my cup in a toast to Trey for a job well done. He and I and my family were pleased to be so close to so much beauty, and I couldn't help but think that Oregon's summer season is really made for moments like this: precious time that's not to be wasted.

As Trey admired the setting, he noted, "When the sun finally breaks through, it does offer an unbelievable vista of Timothy Lake, the forest, and snow-covered Mt. Hood dominating the entire scene. That's one of the things that strikes me the most about this area—plus it's a neat and pristine getaway and such a short hop from Portland."

Timothy Lake is open from May until September. It is one of a few lakes in the Mt. Hood National Forest that allows motorized boating. In addition to fishing, a hiking trail circles the lake and the Pacific Crest National Scenic Trail passes by the east shore. The campground is available by reservation only.

---

12 Timothy Lake Hoodview Campground and Day Use Area

Where: Forest Service Road 57; Latitude: 45.106636, Longitude: -121.783603
Web: fs.usda.gov
Phone: 541-622-7674; 877-444-6777 (reservations)

Summer

Grant McOmie's Outdoor Talk—A Family Who Fishes Together, Stays Together

Have you ever considered the influences that helped you discover the great outdoors? Maybe it was a singular event like a memorable family camping trip or an exciting backpacking adventure with your dad, uncle, or grandparent. Perhaps there was a significant mentor who influenced and introduced you to the wonders of fishing—a friend, a parent, or maybe a grandparent who showed you the way and which end of a fishing rod catches the big ones.

I recently joined a family well familiar with the values of *the family who fishes together, stays together*. The Monroe clan loves to gather for quality time on the water through shared angling adventures. They've been at it for decades so they certainly know how it's done. Bill Monroe, the well-known Oregon outdoor reporter and *Oregonian* newspaper columnist, has written about all things in the great outdoors for nearly 4 decades and said that he looks forward to time on the water with his wife, Glenda, daughter Molly Monroe, and daughter-in-law Kaitlyn Monroe.

His son, Bill Jr., recently let his passion for fishing and the outdoors lead him on a new career path: he is a full-time fishing guide. Bill the younger threaded "plug cut" herring onto barbless (required) hooks. He relies on attractants called "Fish Flash" (in fact, he's recently invented his own color combinations that he uses exclusively on all his rods) that draw fish to the bait through their spinning action. Each angler slowly let the bait and tackle down near the bottom. He chuckled and said, "See how that herring is spinning—that says 'bite me, bite me, bite me!'"

Bill Jr. also noted that fishing on the Columbia River is "a high maintenance fishery that requires a lot of work maintaining the rods," but his techniques can be supereffective. He was right for it didn't take long! "There's a fish," he yelled, as his mother's fishing rod throbbed down and then back up and then down once more. She quickly wrested it from the rod holder and then held on for dear life as the line screamed out of the bait casting reel.

The Monroe ladies certainly know how to put that adage into action! They showed how teamwork can make a difference between success and failure in landing a salmon. Molly and Kaitlyn stood shoulder to shoulder with Glenda—they provided her with both moral and physical help as she fought a hard-charging chinook salmon. Glenda chuckled and told me that when she hooks up with a big fish, it's an "all hands on deck event!" Bill watched his wife wrestle the fish to the net.

Bill Jr. quickly scooped it up and into the boat.

Bill Sr. smiled and showed off the timely writing on his T-shirt logo. It read: "You can't scare me—I have daughters." As a husband, father, and grandfather, he was impressed to have such hard-core female anglers onboard the boat. Bill Jr. added that he knows the secret of women who catch the fish: "It's because women *listen*! I mean really listen. This is a good example!"

Bill's wife, Kaitlyn Monroe, said she joins her husband on the water every chance she gets . . . but admits those chances have gotten slimmer since they started raising a family. Bill and Kaitlyn have two young boys, ages 5 and 3. Still, she loves the unexpected pleasures of fishing more than anything else and the fact that you just never know what you're going to catch: "The rush of hooking and playing a big fish is always fun—it's a feeling that you can't really get anywhere else. It's also family time we have out here—and it's such a unique opportunity in Oregon . . . where else can you go and catch so many big fish?"

With that, Kaitlyn's rod folded over and she was into a chinook too. After a moment, we saw the chrome-sided fish gleam under the surface, just 10 yards from the boat. "Oh, isn't that a beauty? That's a fin-clipped hatchery king—and it's big," said her husband. The fish ran and she reeled at each break in the heart-pounding action. Kaitlyn worked hard to keep the fish close by the boat, never allowing slack line to develop from the fish's erratic yet hard-charging bursts. After 15 minutes, Bill dipped the large net under the salmon.

"That is a beautiful fish," said our guide. "Isn't that something special; just look at the way the light hits the sides of that salmon." It was a gorgeous upriver bright chinook—bound for the Columbia River's upper stretches—hundreds of miles from the estuary. Lots of folks are taking advantage of an astounding summer salmon run up the Columbia River—Bill said there's nothing else like it! "We've got more than a million coho and chinook combined headed upriver. This is salmon-central right here."

Molly Monroe credits her dad for her love of all things outdoors. She said that when she was a kid and Bill went on assignment, she would tag along if it was possible. The lessons that she learned along the way certainly took, for Molly is now a US Fish and Wildlife biologist. "It's not just women who enjoy this kind of adventure—it's young people too," noted Molly. "I've come to learn that youngsters really respond to the outdoors if they're exposed to it. We should instill that enthusiasm for fish and wildlife into our communities and our future generations."

As the flood tide rose, the fish bite became more frequent and Molly's chance at a big king salmon came in a sudden moment of sheer excitement as a huge chinook grabbed her bait and determined it was safer back in the ocean. That's where it headed. "Wow—that fish is on a mission," yelled our skipper. "That's a king, no doubt about it!" I suddenly realized Bill's earlier comment about "good listeners" was in action. He shouted commands to his sister that she obeyed: "Up, up, and over with your rod, Molly! Now, go behind Kaitlyn—that's it, now reel, reel, reel, Molly—hurry, hurry, hurry."

She held complete command over the fish, never gave an inch and soon it was scooped up in our guide's net. Score: Molly one—salmon zero! "You did that well," noted her brother. "That was all you, Molly—good job!" Their father chimed in: "Yeah, that was impressive and the women got all three fish. Women rule!" "That is so true," noted her brother. Bill Sr. watched the entire scene and offered: "Women [who fish] are every bit and maybe more important to the outdoor sports these days . . . because they're the mothers of tomorrow. We need to teach more girls that this is fun and valuable, so they remember it for their own children someday."

"When you teach a kid to fish," added Molly, "they are gaining confidence because they're doing it properly and can be rewarded for the effort. So their enthusiasm goes way up too." "Parents who don't do this sort of thing regularly but would like to actually have lots of options," said Bill Sr. "For example, the Oregon Department of Fish and Wildlife [dfw.state.or.us] offers classes for all sorts of outdoor recreation activities—including fishing and crabbing and clamming. There are clubs and organizations like the NW Steelheaders [nwsteelheaders.org] and the Oregon Bass and Panfish club [obpc0.tripod.com] that offer field trips for beginners—both adults and their children. The Oregon State Marine Board offers a free Columbia and Willamette River Boating Facilities Guide that you can download from their website (oregon.gov/OSMB). It's a valuable resource that will be a good starting point for the newcomer. There are many ways that parents can get their children involved in the outdoors."

It was a day to remember, for soon we all had our limits of fish on a trip guaranteed to provide lasting family memories of exciting times in the Oregon outdoors. Seven chinooks in 4 hours—I can't wait to join this crew again!

July

13

Paddling and Hiking
Sauvie Island

There's no finer way to celebrate summer than the family retreat that's easy to find—mere minutes from Portland—for boaters and hikers alike. You and the kids will feel a million miles away along and on Sauvie Island. My wife, Chris, and I recently joined good friends and longtime paddlers Steve and Bonnie Gibons, plus a half dozen other adventurers, for a daylong kayaking excursion. Many of our fellow paddlers were relative newcomers to this stretch of Multnomah Channel at Scappoose Bay, a place where tide and weather can change in a heartbeat.

Trying something new and risky takes courage, but if you're convinced that it's right for you, the risk can often pay off with unique adventures. On this gentle day, the bay and the nearby Columbia River were smooth and calm, so no need for us to worry. "We're going to paddle out of Scappoose Bay and down the channel," explained Steve Gibons, a former kayaking guide. "Our ultimate goal will be the northern end of Sauvie Island and a beautiful little area called Cunningham Slough. Remember, this is not an Olympic event—it's all about taking our time and enjoying the wildlife that's in the bay itself." It's important to note that while the Cunningham Slough provides easy water kayaking, the Multnomah Channel and Columbia River waters that border the island have significant boat traffic including barges, sailboats, power boats, and oceangoing con-

Be sure to glance overhead where ospreys are a common wildlife feature.

Sea kayaks draw only 4 inches of water so you can paddle into many shallow areas.

tainer ships. Only experienced paddlers should use the channel and river. Sturgeon Lake has a boat ramp and is a great paddling option for families.

Finding a comfort zone on the glassy water came easy on a day that was filled with a warm summertime glory—clear skies, a gentle breeze, and outgoing tide to ease our downriver journey. More importantly, our small group of paddlers seemed to have the river all to ourselves on a stretch of Columbia River backwater that's largely overlooked. "I can't tell you how many times people come out and say, 'I can't believe this is only 25 miles away. I feel like I've gone to someplace that would require days to get to," added Steve.

Sea kayaks draw only 4 inches of water so we had easy access into tiny bays and sloughs that provided the opportunity to see many different wildlife species like herons, eagles, osprey, and black-tailed deer. Bonnie Gibons offered: "Kayaking is the best way to experience wildlife because we are so quiet and can slowly paddle our way up close. Especially in the Sauvie Island-Scappoose Bay area—you can go for miles and miles. It's a kayaking mecca!"

It is certainly that—and much more—a time and a place where nature's touch may restore your soul. If there is a more underrated Oregon state park than Wapato Access Greenway State Park on the 16-mile-long Sauvie Island, I certainly do not know where it's tucked away! Wapato Greenway is 88 acres of natural parkland with 2 miles of level, looped trail that, while not ADA accessible, is manageable and fun for even the smallest or most reluctant children, according to Oregon State Parks Ranger

John Mullen. "To some degree, it's the peacefulness of the place that draws parents and their kids. There's not a lot of hubbub out here and it's close enough to Portland you feel like you're getting away even though you're right next door."

The site was once called "Virginia Lake" but it was renamed when Oregon State Parks took over management in the 1970s. Native Americans knew the place well—they lived in the area by the thousands for as many years and grew the namesake wapato plant. "It's a green arrow-shaped leaf plant that grows in the wetlands," noted Mullen. "Native people would cultivate it by planting the bulbs in dispersed areas. It's been diminished quite a bit by invasive reed canary grass or Himalayan blackberry, but in many of these areas wapato has been coming back."

Wapato blooms with small clusters of white flowers in summer and it was traditionally harvested by Native Americans in the fall. The plant was prized for its tuber—similar to a potato—and was a critical staple item in native people's diets. "It's a lovely viewing platform along the trail that overlooks the water—there's a bench you can sit on too. We also provide a picnic shelter area for a larger group to gather. The trail is really easy to walk," added Mullen. "Basically all you hear are the songbirds or the breeze through the leaves. A great place to visit!"

Be sure to bring your binoculars as the trail winds around Virginia Lake that attracts all manner of waterfowl and even beaver and deer. A bird blind and the viewing platform are positioned along the trail and interpretive signs will help you identify birds you may encounter. It's a great place to picnic, but you may want to bring your own snacks as food choices on the island are limited. No drinking water is available at the park and a primitive restroom is accessible only to hikers or by boat at Hadley's Landing. Parking permits are required to park in all wildlife areas and can be purchased in various locations on the island.

Hurry here soon and discover a state parkland that will fill you with pride for its protection and build your enthusiasm measured by the cheers you'll hear from your family. It's easy to reach and access throughout the year.

13 Sauvie Island Wildlife Area

Where: 18330 NW Sauvie Island Road, Portland, OR 97231

Web: dfw.state.or.us

Phone: 503-621-3488

Watch the Episode: traveloregon.com/SauvieIsland

Kayaking with Kids

Kayaking is a fantastic family activity—it keeps everyone exercising and enjoying the out-of-doors together—a wonderful way to build memories. But anytime you are around water with children, extra caution is in order. The safety tips outlined in chapter 11 apply here too. Be sure you have a well-fitted and appropriate personal floatation device (PFD) for every person participating. If you're a beginner, make a trip with a trained guide or experienced paddler at the helm. A professional guide can offer safety instruction and share her experience of a waterway to make your first tour fun. Swimming and kayaking classes are widely available for all ages. And don't forget canoeing, which can be a stable alternative for young children to ride along.

Keep common-sense considerations in mind too. Know your own limitations and consider whether a 1:1 adult to child ratio might be the safest way to enjoy your paddle trip. Do your homework: know the waterway ahead of time. What is the water depth and temperature? Are you likely to encounter smooth or choppy conditions? Will there be underwater hazards like logs or rocks? Always be mindful of posted warnings and off-limits areas.

Remember to consider what the children might most enjoy about the adventure. Factor in the ability of your least experienced paddler when planning the distance and route. Bring along healthy snacks, plenty of water, extra layers of clothing (quick-dry synthetics are a great option), first aid kit, binoculars for wildlife watching, a dry pack for your phone, and your creativity (this may be a great time to resurrect some of those old camp songs and games). Most of all, enjoy learning something new and experiencing nature together.

14

Two Tickets to Ride

It's rare to combine an Oregon history lesson with outdoor recreation, but in Tillamook County you and the kids can touch history by riding the rails on a unique steam engine train ride. In Garibaldi, the Oregon Coast Scenic Railroad (OCSR) connects passengers with recreation that reaches back more than a century. Each morning, engineer Scott Wickert preps the business end of the OCSR: a Prairie 262 steam engine that roars to life in billowy clouds of steam. The engine was built in 1925, burns recycled motor oil, and is rated to pull 29,000 pounds.

"It's like a big industrial furnace," noted Wickert. "The firebox is surrounded by a water jacket and as it boils, the steam rises and moves through super heater units and then down into the cylinders to move the train."

The railroad takes on passengers at the Garibaldi Depot each day for a 90-minute round-trip ride along the coast. The steam engine pulls three passenger cars (plus the caboose) and that's where you'll find OCSR conductor Tim Thompson. He is usually busy checking passengers and punching their tickets, and he's been at it since 2003 when the OCSR began operation in Tillamook County.

Anyone can be a railroad engineer at the Molalla Train Park.

The first railroad arrived in Tillamook County from the Willamette Valley in 1912.

*The Oregon Coast Scenic Railroad moves along at a mere 10 miles per hour
so you've plenty of time to see the sights.*

It primarily hauled timber but it also brought Portland-area passengers to the beach. Tourists quickly fell in love with the sun, the surf, and the chance to get away from it all, according to local historian Don Best. "There were no roads here, nothing but trails in this area," said Best, a longtime resident whose grandfather arrived in Tillamook County in 1910. "You had to go by wagon up the beach line at low tide to get into this area back then. The train changed everything." Best added that a century ago, the railroad was the popular way to reach Tillamook County's gorgeous sandy beaches and access was convenient. "You could get on the train at 9:30 in Portland and be walking on Rockaway Beach at 2:30 in the afternoon. It was the most accessible beach on the Oregon coast."

People came by the thousands and vacation developments were ready to meet them, boasting familiar sounding names like Manhattan Beach, Brighton Beach, and Saltair. Unlike modern vacations that are measured by a few days of getting away from it all, a century ago most families would travel to Rockaway Beach and stay all summer. There weren't many houses in those early days, but camps with wooden tent frames that lined up next to each other. People bought or brought canvas tents and set up their summer camp. Eventually lots were created and vacation cabins were built.

These days, the OCSR runs three or four times a day along a 3-mile stretch of track from Garibaldi to Rockaway Beach; at 10 miles an hour, it is a pleasant cruise. I chatted with many folks who brought their kids along for the ride—visitor Ahne Oosterhof said that it's a wonderful way to meet history face-to-face—especially for children. "It is a fun way to see things that we all miss from the highway. It's not very fast, but that's kind of nice because it gives me more time to look around."

Train conductor Tim Thompson agreed and offered, "On a hot summer weekend in Portland, we are packed! Folks love the open cars with sunshine and cool breezes, while others choose to sit inside our fully restored Wilson River car and reflect on the history of the railroad. It's a lot of fun for folks who've never experienced an old-fashioned train ride and want to connect with Oregon's past."

There's another link to Oregon's railroading past that the kids will absolutely love and it's not far from Portland. You can tell a lot about a community's health by the parklands they support and in Molalla, Oregon, there is a dandy—where fried chicken and coleslaw are the picnic staples for scores of families and where plenty of elbow room lets the kids play safely. It's also where something special is always comin' 'round the bend at the Molalla Train Park, a private parkland that sprawls across 4 acres in Clackamas County and where seven miniature trains cruise the rails that also allow hundreds of park visitors to go aboard for a 10-minute ride. "It's awesome to see all their smiles, see the excitement, the look in their eyes," said Pat Duling, president and lead engineer for the Pacific Northwest Live Steamers. "Every kid loves trains and most adults do too although they may not admit to it! That's what hooked me at a young age."

The PNW Live Steamers is a train club whose 80 members keep the engines running each week. Their trains are 1.5-inch model scale so big enough for people to sit on, ride, and smile all the way. The Molalla Train Park was the brainchild of founder Harry Harvey who put down the first track in 1954 as a gift to his community. "When Harry started the park," noted Duling, "he wanted it to be free for all people. So if you were less fortunate, you could still come and have a great time and treat your family to an awesome day." And it's still all free—each Sunday—all summer long! Inside the Dennis Jacobs Roundhouse, the members' locomotives are at the ready. Dave Middleton and his son, Troy Middleton, agreed that their hobby is addictive. "This is fun," said Dave, who added with a chuckle, "when it becomes work, it's time to get out of the hobby!"

Back on the railroad, visitors Michelle and Travis Shatto love the railroad's link to childhood because it hit really close to home. "I was 12 the last time I rode," said the beaming Travis. "That's more than 30 years ago when my uncle was a member. He brought us here during the middle of the week and we had the place to ourselves and he ran us around for hours." His wife, Michelle, heartily agreed and added, "It is so scenic and really brings you back to when you were a little kid." The Molalla Train Park is open to engineers of all ages and it will put a smile on your face—guaranteed!

14A Oregon Coast Scenic Railroad

Where: 306 American Avenue, Garibaldi, OR 97118

Web: oregoncoastscenic.org

Phone: 503-842-7972; 888-718-4253

Watch the Episode: traveloregon.com/CoastRailroad

14B Molalla Train Park/Pacific Northwest Live Steamers

Where: 31803 S. Shady Dell Road, Molalla, OR 97038

Web: pnls.org

Phone: 503-829-6866

Watch the Episode: traveloregon.com/MolallaTrain

15

A Butterfly Playground

In the heart of Oregon's summer season, you can find a bit of a blissful time marked by long warm days that invite you to linger longer in the outdoors in one small Oregon town; it's also the busiest time of the year for the flying insects that some say speak to our hearts: butterflies! In Elkton, Oregon, the local residents are doing amazing things to help Oregon's native butterflies through lessons and actions that prove—*if you build the habitat, the butterflies will come.*

The traffic on State Highway 38 speeds by at an ear-shattering rate near Elkton in Douglas County—but step inside the town's Community Education Center and prepare to be amazed. "I think every one of us has a memory of a butterfly dancing across the sky," noted Education Center Director Marjory Hamann. "It's a sense of awe and how our visitors can become still as statues when they have direct engagement with monarch butterflies— it seems to be touching something—perhaps a need to be close to nature—in all of us."

Nature reigns supreme inside the Butterfly Pavilion at the 30-acre Elkton Community Education Center where monarch and painted lady butterflies seem to pose or preen while you are held spellbound watching a butterfly come to life. Grace Whitley, a sophomore at Elkton High School, said that she has learned so much about each butterfly's life since she started working at the center. For

You'll be spellbound watching a monarch butterfly come to life.

example, a butterfly's vision is amazing, for each insect has up to 17,000 eyes. Plus, the tiny insects can see color up to 100 feet away. Whitley and seventeen other local students work at the center following a passion to teach visitors about each phase of butterfly life. "They smell with their antenna, they taste with their feet, and then they eat with their proboscis, which is their tongue," said Whitley with a giggle. "They are fascinating creatures in every phase of their lives."

The Butterfly Pavilion is but one stop at this unique Oregon destination that sprawls across a former sheep pasture. Since 1999, local Elkton residents have transformed the property into a botanical garden that grow scores of butterfly-friendly plants. Other family-friendly amenities at the center include a re-creation of the Hudson's Bay Company's Fort Umpqua (their southernmost outpost in the mid-1800s), a summer café run by area high school students, a gift shop featuring the work of local artists, a library, and art exhibits. The center's hours vary by season, and a calendar of special events on their website might help in your trip planning, but the admission is free. Two years ago, Barb Slott, a retired wildlife biologist, now one of the center's Butterfly Stewards, said that she moved to Elkton after just one visit to the Education Center. Now, she's a regular volunteer—as are scores of other residents. "To come and see this resource in a town of just 200 people just blew me away," noted Slott. "Our community of Elkton is

The Butterfly Pavilion is one of many reasons to stop at the Elkton Community Education Center.

concerned about itself! We want to see this as a place for families and retirees and for businesses to grow."

The center also grows much-in-demand native plants and flowers that you can buy. For example, you will find milkweed that is a host plant for monarchs during their caterpillar phase or the gorgeous perennial flower called bee balm that provides nectar during the monarch's butterfly phase. The Elkton Community Education Center was recently awarded a grant from the Travel Oregon Forever Fund. The generous financial aid will allow the center to grow even more plants for sale and conduct even more workshops for visitors. "It's extremely helpful to have a source of funding that says, 'We'll front you the money first, while you get your legs under you' and then let it be self-sustaining over time," noted Director Hamann. The Elkton Community Education Center is a remarkable example that is built around a simple premise: *a small town can do great big things!*

---

15 Elkton Community Education Center

Where: 15850 State Highway 38 W, Elkton, OR 97436

Web: elktonbutterflies.com

Phone: 541-584-2692

Watch the Episode: traveloregon.com/elktons-butterfly-playground

---

16

Let's Go Outdoors

I t's summertime time and there is a certain shout-out heard far and wide across Oregon that's all about learning new outdoor skills thanks to the Oregon Parks and Recreation Department's program called simply Let's Go. Camping, hiking, crabbing, clamming, paddling, cycling, birding, and even disc golf are but a handful of the experiences you can try in the great outdoors at an Oregon state park near you. For starters, there's an easy, friendly way to learn camping basics on a getaway to several state parks including Silver Falls State Park Campground.

On a recent Saturday morning in mid-July, Eric and Mindy Markman and their young kids hoped to leave all their worries behind on a special campout at

Slide into the cozy confines of a kayak for a paddle across Estacada Lake.

Silver Falls State Park. "First and foremost it's about us getting together as a family on a weekend," noted Eric. "Getting away from the city and getting into nature is a great experience for us too." His wife, Mindy, added, "I want them to have an appreciation for nature and feel like they can set up the tent themselves and that it is fun to go camping."

"Have fun and try not to make too much work" is a key message for the folks who signed up for the Oregon State Parks program called Let's Go Camping. It's a bit like a class in Camping 101 where no assumptions are made about your outdoor

Let's Go Outdoors at Estacada Lake starts with a safety chat on how to paddle.

skills, abilities, or experiences. Former Oregon Parks and Recreation staff member Kevin Farron plus a core volunteer group operate Let's Go Camping seminars for newcomer campers at many state parks through the summer. "First, it's a very close-knit family environment and we're all camping together—but it's not necessarily a summer camp. We don't want parents to come out and unload their kids; that's not the goal of the program." In fact, the goal is to introduce beginners to the techniques and equipment that many car campers (folks who stay in a tent rather than a trailer or RV) might consider for their own camping trip. If you don't own camping gear that's OK because they will loan you the tent, sleeping bags, pads, and stoves to set you on the right path.

Eric said the idea is perfectly suited to families that are trying to get their youngsters outdoors this summer. "If you haven't done much camping and you're a little intimidated by it, it's a great way to start. A low risk, highly educational and great family-oriented approach to doing it." The price is right too! On this weekend, eight families signed up for an overnight session at Silver Falls State Park and each family paid just 30 dollars to go to the camping school. Park rangers also assist the class with lessons on safety. For example—showing and talking about the ten safety essentials you'd want to take with you on a hike. Volunteers also demonstrate and share camping techniques like the proper way to build a fire. Farron said there's even a cooking lesson—Dutch oven style: "Everybody loves

Dutch oven cooking—it's new to most people and you get a tasty treat at the end so it's very interactive. Plus, the kids help out."

Mindy Markman and Whitney Woolf agreed that the benefits for the kids are huge: "The guides help the kids," noted Mindy, a returning student in the camping class. "Our first year they taught us how to fish, showed us how to make a fire using just flint stones, and even took us on guided hikes to learn the varied flora and fauna. All those things are really important to us."

"We live in a neighborhood, which is great," said Whitney. "But I really want my kids to have more wild experiences, so that's what I hope to get out of it —camping in the great outdoors—no fences, just big trees."

Bryan Jones, a Let's Go Camping volunteer, said that as a lifelong Oregon camper, he wouldn't trade a minute of the experiences he's had teaching Oregon's next generation of campers. "I saw this program online and I clicked on the link and volunteered for a weekend to help out—now, I'm hooked on showing inexperienced families the pleasures in our great area that we call Oregon—show them how to set up a tent, how to make a fire, take them on a little nature hike. You can't believe how happy it makes people feel to discover Oregon this way."

"I hope to see the families all leave with smiling faces," added Farron. "I hope they're enthused and excited and return on their own to an Oregon state park. Perhaps they'll discover it's really worth it, that Oregon's outdoors is wonderful."

The Let's Go concept will even teach you more about Oregon history that you can see up close and even touch. For example, you can "find the fort" at Fort Stevens, when you follow Park Ranger John Koch through a locked gate and into the darkness for a stroll underground on a free guided tour of Battery Mishler. It's chilly, damp, and dimly lit, but a place where you can touch Oregon's military past. A century ago, Battery Mishler was a part of the Columbia River Harbor Defenses system that included multiple gun batteries located on both sides of the Columbia River. At Fort Stevens, Battery Mishler was the only underground battery and it housed two 10-inch guns that were open to the sky. Each gun was mounted on disappearing carriages, which hid the guns behind concrete and earth walls when not being fired. The guns could fire 617-pound shells at a distance of 9 miles.

The tour takes you past hallways and rooms and interesting features including a massive underground gun pit. The huge gun was mounted atop a large, thick concrete pillar. Koch added, "You get a feel for the grit of the work and what the environment was like for the soldiers down here. You can't duplicate this anywhere else—you can only get it at Fort Stevens. You're not going to see this anywhere in the United States—only here in Oregon."

Chris Havel, spokesperson for Oregon State Parks, said that the Let's Go Outdoors program began in 2000 and it was born with just one event and a simple idea: "Back then we asked ourselves, what is it we do best to bring families out? Well, we introduce them to camping—that's really our bread and butter. So that's how it began, but it wasn't long and we asked why is it just camping? Not everyone can get away for a night. So that's when Let's Go really took off."

I'll say—today, there are scores of events that take place at state parks across Oregon. The activities are affordable, easy, and teach you something new, like a paddle trip across Estacada Lake at Milo McIver State Park in Clackamas County. In fact, we recently joined a small group of first-time paddlers and lead guide Andrew Brainard. The park provided the paddles, the life vests, super stable flat water kayaks for each paddler, and plenty of solid instruction. "Estacada Lake is calm water, there are no obstacles for us so it's a leisurely place to paddle," noted Brainard. The idea of this Let's Go program is to give the novice kayak user an introduction to kayaking and a chance to experience the Clackamas River watershed from a different point of view.

First-time paddler Krys Smith said she fell in love with the lake, the boats, and her chance to try something new: "Oh, this is really good for me—I like it a lot and I think I'm going to try more kayaking—Andrew is really patient too and takes his time with each of us." Smith said she was also impressed that the lake and the park are only 45 minutes from downtown Portland and yet, a world away from the city tumult and noise.

The Let's Go program is paying off too—visitor day use and overnight campouts have climbed as much as 15 percent at some state parks each year over the past 8 years. "There are a lot of ways to enjoy being in Oregon and this is one of the best," said Havel. "This is as close to the Oregon experience as you can get and a lot of people move here dreaming that they're going to do something like this, but they don't know how to take that first step! For many people, this is the first step and once they do they are off and going." You'll be going too! Let's Go is open to everyone, but for birding, paddling, and disc golf, children need to be at least 8 years old. Camping and hiking are available for all ages. And with the exception of camping and paddling, most Let's Go activities are free of charge. The wealth of Let's Go Outdoors adventures is too hard to resist—so check them out and get outdoors soon.

Let's Go Camping

Where: various parks throughout the state
Web: oregonstateparks.org
Phone: 888-953-7677 (Oregon State Parks Reservation Center)

16A Silver Falls State Park

Where: 20024 Silver Falls Highway SE, Sublimity, OR 97385
Web: oregonstateparks.org
Phone: 503-873-8681; 800-551-6949

16B Fort Stevens State Park

Where: 100 Peter Iredale Road, Hammond, OR 97121
Web: oregonstateparks.org
Phone: 503-861-3170 x21; 800-551-6949

16C Milo McIver State Park

Where: 24101 S Entrance Road, Estacada, OR 97023-9675
Web: oregonstateparks.org
Phone: 503-630-7150; 800-551-6949

Watch the Episodes: traveloregon.com/UndergroundFtStevens *and* traveloregon.com/LetsGoOutdoors

August

17

Monumental Reflection at Newberry National Volcanic Monument

When I was a boy I fell in love with long distance—not the telephone kind, but the dust-filled lanes and rambling asphalt roads that enticed a small-town kid from central Oregon to explore his home region more than 40 years ago. These roads invited me to roam Oregon's remote alpine mountains, glacier-fed rivers, and nearly 400 miles of Pacific shoreline.

A small army of long-ago authors named Stevenson, Kipling, Verne, and London fueled a burning desire in me for distant places first sparked by a hard-working grandfather. I also admired and looked to my grandfather for inspiration and lessons about fishing, hiking, camping, and exploring the country beyond my own backyard.

Some of my earliest memories center on family campouts along a lake-shore—perhaps Paulina Lake or East Lake in the central Oregon Cascades, where I would lie at night, wrapped by starlight and spellbound by my grandfather's tales of big fish and elusive bull elk. In the early morning light, I'd awaken to the crackle and hiss of a warming fire, poke my head out of the snug sleeping bag, and gaze across a shimmering lake surface reflecting a million blinding suns rising above the caldera of the burned-out volcano called Newberry Crater.

I can still hear the laughter and banter of half a dozen siblings and same-aged cousins who grew up with me. Like a band of backwoods troopers, we marched and played across our Deschutes National Forest wilderness or sat motionless for hours, eyes transfixed by the twitching tip of a fishing rod, as though willpower alone could make a hesitant trout bite the bait. We believed the Oregon outdoors was ours for the taking and enjoying, that our times together would last forever.

The view atop Paulina Peak to the Newberry Crater is awe-inspiring.

Summer and fall camping trips that centered on fishing or hunting were my grandfather's way of teaching me about the outdoors—and, the fact is, he knew his stuff. He'd grown up working and exploring and playing throughout much of Oregon some 50 years earlier, and while camping was an affordable option for many families of limited means, I think his real intent was to instill self-reliance and confidence in the young ones. Camping adventures certainly did that, but they also gave me a sense of place and family that didn't fully register until much later in my life when my three sons were of an age to understand and appreciate time spent in the Oregon outdoors.

My wife, Chris, and I started them young too, always on the go and ever-ready to break out of the school routine and troop along with their folks as soon as possible. When the mood to move struck us, there seemed no better way to celebrate summer than packing up and moving out toward our annual camping adventure at East or Paulina Lakes. We'd leave busy US 97 near Bend behind and follow the lonesome trail high into the alpine reaches of Newberry National Volcanic Monument.

Created in 1990, Newberry includes over 50,000 acres of lakes, lava flows, and spectacular geologic features. Named for Dr. John S. Newberry, a scientist and early explorer with the Pacific Railroad Survey, the caldera (the center of the volcano) holds two lakes, Paulina Lake and East Lake. The monument's summit is 7,985-foot Paulina Peak, which offers showcase views of the Oregon Cascades and the high desert. It's hard to believe as you drive through this mountainous area that you are within the caldera of a 500-square-mile volcano that remains very active seismically and geothermally to this day. Geologists believe the park sits over a shallow magma body only 2 to 5 kilometers deep. Retired geologist Bob Jensen noted, "Probably the most spectacular views you can find are atop Paulina Peak! On a clear day you can see from Washington's Mt. Adams to California's Mt. Shasta—and to the east you can see all the way to distant Steens Mountain."

Every direction you look is a recreation heaven on earth offering snowcapped peaks, deep green forests, inviting pockets of ponds, and grassy meadows. Down closer to ground, stop in at nearby Lava Butte and discover that all of this region's geologic history is a part of the remarkable Newberry Monument. "A key place to start is probably the Lava Lands Visitor Center," added Jensen. "You get a handle on the big story of what happened in Central Oregon as recently as a thousand years ago. There is also the great viewpoint atop Lava Butte that overlooks the area. Then the Lava River Cave is nearby and easy to explore in summer. It's the longest lave tube in the state." The center is open from May to December and hours vary. It houses films and hands-on exhibits on the geological history of the area to interest children of all ages, a bookstore, restrooms, and a 3D topographical map, and is surrounded by trails for hiking and biking. During the summer you can even pay a small fee for a shuttle van that will take you round-trip from the Visitor Center to the summit of Lava Butte. Note that recreation parking passes are required here from May 1 to September 30 and can be purchased on-site. If you go caving, be prepared with a lantern and dress for warmth because even on the hottest summer day, inside Lava River Cave it's a constant 42 degrees.

Scott McBride, former national monument manager, said that visitors to this national treasure can spend weeks exploring the monument's 50,000 acres and never see the same thing twice: "Visitors who take the time to turn off Highway 97 are completely surprised by what they almost missed—and then—completely excited that they didn't. It is the easy access to volcanic features, the types of recreation that you can do in the center of a caldera, which is essentially the heart of a massive volcano spreading out the size of Rhode Island."

The caldera also includes the Big Obsidian Flow, deposited 1,300 years ago by an eruption. The obsidian flow is over a mile in length and 200 feet deep, with huge chunks of obsidian scattered about like so many forgotten children's toys. The mile-long stroll puts you in the heart of gray pumice, brick red lava, and ebony obsidian, and the contrasting shapes and colors rest side by side. Bart Wills, then

No tent? That's OK! Enjoy your stay at East Lake in one of their many shoreline rental cabins.

a US Forest Service (USFS) geologist at Newberry Monument, said that Native Americans discovered the glasslike qualities of the obsidian and hand-tooled it into razor-sharp tools for hunting and cleaning game: "It's sharp like glass and it's very brittle; it holds a keen edge but it breaks very easily. So once you've obsidian as a tool—say, an arrow, the tip may break and they wouldn't be able to use it again. But—as you can see—there was no shortage of material."

Today the fractured, jagged ramparts of the volcano are topped by the pinnacle called Paulina Peak, but a glance down to Paulina or East Lake's forested shore always reminds me of my true interest in this site, and it won't take long for you to discover that camping has long been a tradition here. East Lake is an Oregon destination with unmatched Cascade Mountain scenery and where warm hospitality is king—it's a timeless place perfect for building lasting family memories of camping together in the great outdoors. East Lake anglers have enjoyed a summer trout-fishing heritage that reaches back more than a century; anglers travel to the pristine lake to fish for rainbow trout, brown trout, and kokanee.

The first East Lake Resort was built in 1915, according to resort co-owner, Bruce Bronson. He told me with a chuckle, "A lot of people walk in the front door and ask, 'Where is the caldera? I came here to see the Newberry Caldera.' . . . Well, you're in it." Bronson added that East Lake has long been a drawing card for the angling crowd, especially at daybreak when trout and kokanee are on the bite. "Families have been coming here since the very beginning when it took much longer to get here, but then they stayed much longer too. Many came up as children;

they'll come up with pictures of themselves in front of these same cabins when they were 5 or 6 years old and say, 'Boy, it hasn't changed much. Just like I remember.'"

East Lake Resort's cabins offer all the comforts of home—just like the cozy café where no one ever walks away hungry. Rental boats put you on the water where fishermen troll or cast flies that entice big fish to bite. Nearby, two USFS campgrounds called East Lake and Cinder Hill offer more than 150 campsites for tent or trailer with plenty of lakeshore elbow room that will find you coming back to Newberry again and again. "People have a super outdoor experience in an atmosphere so clean and clear at 6,400 feet in elevation that the clouds seem but an arm's length away," added Bronson. "Laid-back is a great way to describe our place. It's for people who really want to get away from the hustle and bustle of their city lives. They come up here and—within a day or two—all that they thought was so important seems to disappear."

That's certainly true! The stress melts away. There is no water-skiing or jet skiing on either Paulina or East Lakes, so life moves here at a slower pace. "It's the camping, the hiking, fishing, and horseback riding," noted Scott McBride. "Almost anything you can think of to do recreationally, we have it here in this national monument and that is extraordinary."

**17A Deschutes National Forest
Cascades Lakes Welcome Station**

Where: 63095 Deschutes Market Road, Bend, OR 97701
Web: fs.fed.us
Phone: 541-383-5300

17B Lava Lands Visitor Center

Where: 58201 US 97, Bend, OR 97707
Web: fs.usda.gov
Phone: 541-593-2421

17C East Lake Resort

Where: 22430 Paulina Lake Road, La Pine, OR 97739
Web: eastlakeresort.com
Phone: 541-536-2230

Watch the Episode: traveloregon.com/newberrycrater

Family Camping Basics

Camping is a great way to take a break from your family's day-to-day routine, to find a few moments together free from technology and scheduled activities, and to reconnect with nature and with each other. If you're new to camping, the prospect can seem daunting, but resources abound to help you get started. Sign up for a class like the one outlined in chapter 16: The "Let's Go Camping!" series sponsored by the Oregon Department of Fish and Wildlife each summer includes hands-on lessons, nature hikes, and fun family activities that will give you solid footing to explore camping on your own. Or team up with an experienced family for an overnight or two together and let them show you the ropes. In my experience, people who are passionate about camping also love to introduce new folks to this wonderful world. Or consider a practice campout in your own backyard—this is a fun way to test the waters without being too far from familiar comforts for the little ones.

Before you venture out, consider what kind of camping might be the most fun for your family. Car camping, where you can park your car right next to the campsite, is a family favorite because it gives you ready access to all your supplies. Many of these campgrounds have restrooms and shower facilities and even recreational activities and barbecues at the ready. This works especially well for families with young children.

Don't feel compelled to spend a fortune on equipment for your first venture. Ask around and see if you can borrow essential items from friends or family. Or check into whether your campsite might have equipment available to rent.

Be sure to plan ahead to avoid disappointment. Reserve a camp spot early. Oregonians love to camp and many popular campgrounds fill up quickly when the reservation lines open. When the camping date arrives be sure to leave home early enough to arrive at your campsite while it's still daylight. Unpacking and raising a tent in the dark can be trying, even for experienced campers.

Key items to bring when camping with kids include:

- **Plenty of food**—and you don't have to relegate yourself to hot dogs and s'mores. Think creatively. I've known families to whip up a dinner of pasta, garlic bread, and salad at the campsite—real comfort food in the outdoors. Try your hand at Dutch oven cooking before your first trip; masterful meals can come from this traditional camping pot.

- **Plenty of water**—check with your campground to see if potable water is available on-site. If not, bring water from home and have a plan for refilling your containers.

- **All-weather layers**—weather can be unpredictable and even in our Oregon summer rain can fall; be sure to pack lightweight, synthetic layers for warmth and waterproofing. Avoid natural fibers like cotton and wool that stay wet for long periods of time.

- **Emergency supply kit**—first aid items, bug spray, sunscreen. Consider your campsite and activities when outfitting your kit: what hazards might you encounter? Poison oak? Fish hooks? Bug bites? Campfire burns? Think through the possibilities and bring appropriate supplies.

- **And above all, a good attitude**—part of what makes camping special is "roughing it" together with your family. Expect challenges and plan to greet them with a cooperative attitude. Modeling creative problem-solving for your kids might result in some of your favorite memories.

Popular campsites require a reservation so I encourage folks to consider reserving their sites a least 6 months out.

18

Mt. Hood History and Huckleberry Harvest

E arly morning—when air is cool and scenery quiet—Mt. Hood is a marvel! It's my favorite time of day to get a jump start at a place that is filled with adventures. I like to think of Mt. Hood as Portland's hip-pocket mountain where you can discover a unique chapter of Oregon history and an early season huckle-berry harvest. First stop is Government Camp—one of many small villages that ring the Mt. Hood region, but this one offers a fine drop-in site so you can get your bearings at the Mt. Hood Cultural Center and Museum.

"Our mission is to preserve the history of Mt. Hood," said Cheryl Maki, the museum's manager. "We've got ski history, pioneer history, 10th Mountain Division history, the mountain's geologic history, and more." Climb the stairs to the second floor inside the massive 9,000-square-foot museum and discover a unique chapter of the Mt. Hood lifestyle that dates to the 1920s. It was a time and place when an enduring recreation era began—when Henry Steiner began building log cabins across the forest.

This was a time long before electric tools, so hand tools like a froe (on display and you can actually hold it) were used for splitting shingles and shakes. It was work that demanded certain expertise. Henry Steiner and his sons delivered plenty of hand-built craftsmanship through their 30-plus years of mountain cabin con-struction. Namely, longevity! There are more than 100 Steiner cabins still standing in the forest today. The remarkable wooden structures are kept in tip-top shape by folks who enjoy holding on to heritage.

The Mt. Hood Cultural Center and Museum offers a walking tour of eight Steiner Cabins each year—the event is held on the second weekend in August and

I am an unabashed "huckleberry hound" when the huckleberries are ripe.

is fine way to learn more about the history of the Mt. Hood area. In addition, the center can link you with more information on renting cabins—including many of the historic Steiner cabins that are available as rentals. "The cabin owners are very proud of them," added Maki. "Some people have bought the cabins and restored them to their original glory. For so many log cabins to be around after so many decades is pretty impressive."

In August, the Mt. Hood National Forest is where quiet back roads lead me to delicious rewards during what my family affectionately calls, "huckleberry hound time." US Forest Service (USFS) spokesperson Jennifer O'Leary said that huckleberry picking is "a wonderful activity to enjoy with family or friends. It's really great to see the kids out there enjoying themselves and tasting a little bit of Mother Nature."

First stop is the Estacada Ranger Station for a free personal use permit. The permit explains the rules for gathering berries and where you can or cannot pick berries (for example, all wilderness areas are off-limits). I drive an hour from Estacada to reach our huckleberry heaven along USFS Road #42 (Skyline Road). This is an area we have explored countless times through the years. Our favorite areas include the Memaloose and Hillockburn side roads. Bring a forest map as the #42 road does go through areas on non-Forest Service land. To maximize the enjoyment of your berry-picking experience with children, be sure everyone is wearing sturdy, closed-toe shoes and has their legs covered (pants or long socks) to avoid scratches. Bring manageable-sized containers with handles for collecting the berries and perhaps a larger bucket in the car so you can go back for more if you find an especially prolific patch. Bug spray and sunscreen are a good idea too and remember you'll be off the beaten path, so restrooms will likely be unavailable. Bring extra food and water and tell someone where you are going, as there is no phone service. Finally, be diligent about your surroundings; it's easy to be so engrossed in berry picking that you wander off the trail and get lost. And if you're berry hunting in an area known for bears, just make plenty of noise by clapping and talking to avoid unwanted encounters.

I usually just pull over at a clearing thick with purple wildflowers and coniferous trees here and there. Nine species of huckleberries grow in the forest, but two dominate this area: one is large and sweet, the other is redder and more tart. Huckleberries are similar in appearance to blueberries. We have no trouble finding plenty of bushes full of berries that are a bit like candy drops. I usually eat more than I pick as the berries are plentiful, especially in areas of the forest that provide a sun–shade mix. If you lift up a branch and expose the underside, you'll find an easier chore of picking the berries, especially if you have both hands free. O'Leary advised that newcomers "get out into the forest and explore because there are many roads where there are huckleberry patches nearby . . . if you see a huckleberry bush by the side of the road, chances are good there's more right there, so get out there and look."

Soon, we are kitchen-bound with our bounty to prepare a favorite family recipe called Huckleberry Crisp. It's a simple recipe (see page 107) that works well with the tart berries and best of all, it can be assembled and cooked in less than an hour.

18A Mt. Hood Cultural Center and Museum

Where: 88900 Government Camp Loop, Government Camp, OR 97028
Web: mthoodmuseum.org
Phone: 503-272-3301
Watch the Episode: traveloregon.com/huckleberryhounds

18B Estacada Ranger Station

Where: 595 NW Industrial Way, Estacada, OR 97023
Web: fs.usda.gov
Phone: 503-630-6861

Watch the Episode: traveloregon.com/Huckleberryhounds

Huckleberry Crisp

Filling:

⅓ cup sugar

2 tablespoons cornstarch

¼ teaspoon cinnamon

¼ teaspoon nutmeg

¼ teaspoon salt

1 tablespoon lemon juice

1 cup huckleberry or blueberry juice

4 cups huckleberries
   (slightly sweetened)

Topping (recipe follows)

Topping:

⅓ cup butter

1 cup brown sugar

2 tablespoons flour

3 cups corn flakes

Preheat oven to 400°F.

For the filling:

Combine sugar, cornstarch, cinnamon, nutmeg, and salt in a saucepan. Add lemon and huckleberry juices and stir until smooth. Cook, stirring constantly over low heat for 2 minutes until thickened and clear. Add and thoroughly mix in 4 cups of huckleberries.

Pour filling mixture into a greased baking dish.

For the topping:

Melt butter in a saucepan. In a small bowl, combine brown sugar and flour.

Add the sugar mixture to the melted butter. Cook, stirring constantly over low heat for 3 minutes. Add corn flakes, mixing quickly until they are coated with syrup.

For assembly and baking:

Evenly distribute the topping over the huckleberry filling. Place into preheated oven for no more than 30 minutes until the topping is crispy and crunchy and golden brown.

There you have it: as simple as can be and a delicious reward for time well spent in the great Oregon outdoors. Serves up to eight people.

19

You'll Dig
Oregon's State Gem

O regon's high desert is a vast stretch of the state where distances are great and people are few—and if you know where to look, there are remarkable treasures waiting to be found. When the Spectrum Sunstone Mine rock hopper fills up and the generator fires up, the conveyor belt gets your hopes up: Oregon's state gem, the sunstone, will roll past you by the hundreds. The Spectrum Sunstone Mine is located 30 miles northwest of Plush, Oregon, and you'll want to bring a bucket to hold the sunstone riches you find in this pocket of the high desert.

Sunstone Mine manager Jessica Schenk said, "It's very quiet out here and it's very rural so be ready for that—plus, there's no shade whatsoever so bring a sun hat, gloves, water, and a bucket to carry your sunstones back home." Chris Rose— owner and operator of the Spectrum Mine, said that he's been working his claim for more than 12 years. He showed us how easy it is to find them. In a matter of minutes, he worked the soft dirt with a rock pick and pried a gorgeous 25-carat red sunstone from a 6-foot-deep sunstone pit. He noted that the "redder the sunstone, the more valuable the sunstone."

"Now, these are cuttable stones [they can be faceted and polished by a jeweler] and they'll be worth $100 a carat. This one is about 25 carats and is pretty rough but after being cut and cleaned it will probably be about a 5-carat gem—not bad, eh?" Not bad at all! The Spectrum Sunstone Mine is open to the public and for a fee, you can scoop up shovel loads of sunstone rich ore, dump each onto a screen, and shake away the dirt to find the stones.

That's the technique Colleen Schlosser and young Jonah Luedecke chose after they traveled to the Spectrum Mine from Portland—in fact, it was their third

Treasure hunting for sunstones is a terrific parent-child camping adventure.

visit of the summer to explore and dig sunstones! We watched as Jonah found a dandy sunstone in minutes. It shimmered in the brilliant sunshine and showed off a golden hue. Schlosser didn't mind the Southeast Oregon remoteness or the summer heat that rose to the high 90s across a rugged countryside that few folks visit. "Oh, not at all—this is great mother-son camping time and we are treasure hunting. It's exciting because you are constantly picking sunstones from the ore that Chris digs up for us—plus, these are state gemstones after all and that's fun too. I love Oregon and it's cool to bring home buckets of the state gem to show off to our friends and family—and I craft jewelry with them."

Sunstones are copper-laden crystals that formed tens of millions of years ago—the crystals flowed to the surface with volcanic magma and are concentrated in this part of Southeast Oregon. It's the microscopic copper bits that give sunstones their color—that color ranges from light champagne to ruby red. Schlosser's love for Oregon's sunstone is reflected in gorgeous jewelry that she creates in her Portland studio. "I really love what I'm doing—what I'm working on—I love the tools and the stones and the metal—it all has so much history to it and I think that's exciting."

She says her love for rockhounding began as a child when she collected agates. That passion has melded with her love for crafting artistic pieces. Her company Wirestone Jewelry (etsy.com/shop/Wirestone) offers silver-wrapped creations from earrings to pendant necklaces where stunning sunstones are center stage. "They're always beautiful," said Schlosser. "Sometimes you'll get chips and inclusions and whatnot, but you can tumble those and they become gorgeous. People love the tumbled stones too."

She calls the smaller stones "drops of honey" and their rich colors really shine. The fact that she has dug the gems herself fills her with pride. In fact, she and her son cannot wait for summer to arrive so they can return for more adventure in the Oregon desert. "It's a 7-hour drive and I enjoy it. It's the desert; the smell of it, the mountains—it's quiet. The whole thing is really just a fun trip."

Mining for sunstones is an exciting adventure because you just never know what you are going to find and it's so easy anyone can try. "The word is getting out and more people show up each summer," said Schenk. "Visitors don't mind the long drive from the Willamette Valley because it's so beautiful out here and the sunstones are gorgeous too. Every Oregonian should have an Oregon sunstone!"

The Spectrum Sunstone Mine is open daily and their season runs from May to November. In addition, the Spectrum Mine is located near a Bureau of Land Management public sunstone site where you are able to dig and keep any sunstones that you find for free. All ages can participate; kids 12 years old and younger dig for free, but it's important to note that the sunstone area is extremely remote— 30 miles of gravel road from the closest town of Plush, Oregon. So be sure you carry extra food and water and be prepared for an emergency. For the dig, you'll also need to bring a shovel, hammer, screwdrivers, bucket, and plastic bags (for the sunstones). Sorting screens are available to borrow or purchase at the mine. Pets on a leash are welcome too. You can camp at the mine (no electricity hookups) or contact them ahead of time for availability of their cabins or 20-foot tepee with fire pit. Restrooms and hot showers are also available.

---

19 Spectrum Sunstone Mine

Where: Latitude: N 42 43.941; Longitude: W 119 52.007;
    a map and detailed directions are available on their website.
Web: highdesertgemsandminerals.com
Phone: 775-772-7724; 775-830-5797
Watch the Episode: traveloregon.com/sunstones

20

Oregon's Floating Museum

Not so many decades ago, before there was an interstate highway built of concrete and asphalt, Oregon's commerce moved on liquid highways like the Willamette and Columbia Rivers. While those distant days have passed, it's still possible—in fact, it's rather easy, for you and the kids to reconnect with Oregon's maritime past and have a great adventure along the way. Step aboard the sternwheeler *Portland* and let your imagination guide you on a river cruise to help answer one important question: "If you don't know where you've come from, how will you know where you're going?" It's a fair question that was posed by Bob Hrdlicka, Oregon Maritime Museum history buff and a volunteer guide. He added that nearly 70 years ago, the sternwheeler *Portland* was built to earn her keep at a time when the city of Portland's waterfront was surging with commerce. "Whenever a cargo ship came up along a dock on the Portland waterfront, this sternwheeler had the power to assist it to the dock or pull the ship away from the dock and turn it around on its own length."

Maritime Museum volunteer Ron Youngman knows every square inch of the steam-powered *Portland,* stem to stern, so he's a good man to show you how it all works—like the diesel-fired boilers that produce 1,800 horsepower. The boilers generate enough steam (254 psi) to move 26-inch steel pistons that push two 9-foot-long connecting rods that make the gigantic 25-foot paddlewheel go round and round. Youngman said that the sternwheeler *Portland* is the only ship of its kind in the country: "It's true and really there are very few working steamships in today's world."

In fact, the sternwheeler *Portland* shouldn't be here either! Back in 1981, a handful of volunteers found her in a wrecked heap—parts and pieces strewn across

The sternwheeler Portland *is a living history museum with lessons for kids of all ages.*

the Portland waterfront. But the volunteers were inspired to save her and stepped up with countless hours of labor and raised nearly a million dollars to restore the city's namesake sternwheeler that was built by the Port of Portland in 1947. Today, volunteers like Jim Spitzer feel proud of all that has been accomplished to bring the sternwheeler *Portland* back to life on the water. "I think each of us owes some kind of payback to their community and while lots of people do that in many social ways, I think preserving history is part of that payback too."

Today, the sternwheeler *Portland* is a floating museum that is moored in Portland's Waterfront Park and open 3 days a week for tours and to view the onboard exhibits and museum store. Youngsters are welcome and the steamer even has a designated Children's Corner with interesting nautical objects that kids can touch and operate including a loud ship's whistle. Beyond the Children's Corner, many of the artifacts are fragile and off-limits for handling. Safety is a priority onboard the tug and because some railings are low, adults are asked to keep a close eye on children. The main deck is ADA accessible, but other areas can only be reached by stairs. Children under age 6 are granted free admission. Allow at least 45 minutes to tour the whole tug. And if you really want a complete experience, the tug cruises along the Willamette several times each year for half-day tours. Advanced reservations are required for this adventure.

Captain Clark Carthill is proud to guide passengers on these half-day tours. "Sternwheeler *Portland* developed because of the city's waterfront and Oregon's commerce," Carthill said. "This [Willamette River] was the highway and this was transportation that allowed the city to become the Portland we know today."

That fact—plus the scenery—are not lost on visitors like Sandra Pearce who enjoyed seeing the city from a different point of view: "I love it! When I heard the public can go on a short half-day cruise, I had to take it for a once-in-a-lifetime opportunity. It's relaxing too because you can't think about anything else—almost meditative."

Volunteer Bob Waldron, an Oregon history buff, said the Oregon Maritime Museum keeps the sternwheeler *Portland*'s working history stories alive. Whether outdoors on its decks or indoors, visitors will find exhibits, photos, and models that show you how steam-powered shipping was the foundation of Oregon's economy. "Timber, agricultural products or any kind of raw resource materials, crops, or goods that came out of the Willamette Valley had to come to Portland. The most economical way to get it to other markets was shipping on this superhighway and ships like the *Portland* made that happen. I think the best part is that it's still here. That is worth a pause to consider."

---

20 Oregon Maritime Museum/Sternwheeler *Portland*

Where: On the Willamette River in Waterfront Park; off Naito Parkway at
   Pine Street, Portland, OR 97204

Web: oregonmaritimemuseum.org

Phone: 503-224-7724

September

21

Off-Road Riders

I t's a cool and cloudy morning at Roger's Camp in the Tillamook State Forest, a key staging area for people who like to travel off-road. I've journeyed into the heart of the forest at the invitation of a familiar face and avid off-roader: my brother, Mark McOmie. My brother's off-road recreation is more than a hobby—it's a passion that has shaped much of his outdoor travel and recreation plans. It's also been something that he's shared with his entire family for nearly 30 years.

"ATVing is a great family sport," Mark explained. "It's a super opportunity to get together and explore the outdoors. It's the reason I introduced my sons, Alec and Sean, to the sport at an early age. I think most of the fellows in our party probably have multiple uses for their machines—part workhorse, part recreation vehicle. In fact, I started riding in the early '90s while on hunting trips and it's taken off from there." Recently, several of Mark's friends joined him for a ride across designated trails in the state forest. They certainly have plenty of trails to choose from for our day's adventure.

Jahmaal Rebb, a former ATV specialist with the Oregon Department of Forestry, said that there are more than 250 miles of ATV trails across the Tillamook State Forest. Rebb manages the trails and the riders who travel in the forest and he noted that there's a "dedicated following" of riders who come to play on the state forestland. "This is a community that's been very active since the 1930s—really, since the first Tillamook Burn. Motorized recreation is a big deal here and the folks still come here, put in time on varied projects to improve trails and improve access—they really have a passion for play."

There are three primary off-highway vehicle (OHV) riding areas available in

ATV quads are quick to respond, easy to steer, and surprisingly comfortable.

the forest including Browns Camp (generally open early April through October), Jordan Creek (open Memorial Day through mid-September), and Diamond Mill (open all year). A wide variety of trails provides access into some of the more remote and scenic parts of the forest and provides challenge and excitement for both beginners and experts. You can pick up trail maps at the Tillamook Forest Center. Call the Department of Forestry to check for seasonal or fire restriction trail closures. "We offer a very extensive network of trails," said Rebb. "Scores of off-road trails are a part of a multiuse recreation system. So you must expect to encounter quads, motorbikes, and full-sized four-wheel drives out here." So what is it like to climb aboard and grab on to the steering of a powerful ATV four-wheel-drive quad? In a word—amazing! They are quick to respond, easy to steer, and surprisingly comfortable too.

Steve Lewis, a veteran rider with close to 30 years of riding experience in the state forest, said, "For those who like to go to an amusement park and ride a roller coaster—well, that's what it's like only you are in the woods and you're in total control of the machine. It is also recreation where risk and danger wait at every turn, so safety and common sense and controlling your speed are critical."

That's where recently adopted rules for youngsters come in. Oregon law requires anyone under the age of 16 operating an ATV on public lands to be supervised by an adult over the age of 18. Also, anyone under the age of 18 must wear a helmet and have the chin strap fastened. Youth under the age of 16 are required to have online safety training and all operators of quads and three-wheel ATVs (Class I ATVs) and off-road motorcycles (Class III ATVs) must have an ATV Safety Education Card when operating on lands open to public use. In order to make training as convenient as possible, the Oregon Parks and Recreation Department (OPRD) offers free safety education programs and certification online (rideatvoregon.org). See pages 117–18 for ATV safety details.

21A Jordan Creek

Where: Turnoff is at milepost 18 along Highway 6
Web: rideatvoregon.org
Phone: 503-815-7024 (ODF Tillamook Office);
503-359-7463 (ODF Forest Grove Office)

21B Diamond Mill

Where: Turnoff is at milepost 22.17 along Highway 6
Web: rideatvoregon.org
Phone: 503-815-7024 (ODF Tillamook Office);
503-359-7463 (ODF Forest Grove Office)

21C Browns Camp

Where: Turnoff is at milepost 33 along Highway 6
Web: rideatvoregon.org
Phone: 503-815-7024 (ODF Tillamook Office);
503-359-7463 (ODF Forest Grove Office)

21D Tillamook Forest Center

Where: 45500 Wilson River Highway, Tillamook, OR 97141
Web: tillamookforestcenter.org
Phone: 503- 815-6800; 866-930-4646

Watch the Episode: traveloregon.com/offroadriders

ATVing
with Children

Between 2005 and 2011, 7 children under the age of 15 were killed (per Oregon Center for Health Statistics data) and 108 were injured in Oregon due to nonstandard transportation methods, the majority of these being ATVs. Additionally, 7 percent of all ATV deaths in Oregon occurred in children under the age of 15 and 33 percent for those under 25 (per Oregon Center for Health Statistics data). There has been a large increase in the number of both ATV and off-road two-wheeled motorcycle riders requiring treatment in Oregon's trauma centers. The growing number of ATV-related deaths and injuries are attracting attention both in Oregon and nationally. The number of people who are killed and injured in ATV crashes continues to grow, but crash reports indicate that nearly all these incidents are preventable.

All riders must have an ATV Safety Education Card. The goal of online ATV safety education is to develop safe, responsible riding behaviors to reduce ATV-related deaths and injuries in Oregon. There is no minimum age to take the online course, though some children may have a difficult time with the course material. The Oregon Parks and Recreation Department (OPRD) strongly encourages parents to go through the course materials and test with their child/children. One parent may sign up with up to four kids under a family account and all will be issued cards upon passing the test. Adults supervising youth must also have the card. At the completion of this online course, youth can print a 6-month Certificate of Completion to practice riding, which gives them plenty of time to find a training course (a link to these courses is provided on the rideatvoregon. org website).

The Oregon State Parks and Recreation Department offers free safety education programs online.

Youth under age 16 have the additional requirement to get hands-on training. The ATV *RiderCourse* provides a fast-paced, half-day, hands-on training session that includes pre-ride inspection, starting and stopping, quick turns, hill riding, emergency stopping, and swerving and riding over obstacles. You'll also learn about protective gear, local regulations, places to ride, and environmental concerns. Bring your friends and family, and meet new friends to ride with. All students must, at a minimum, have a properly fitting DOT- (or Snell) approved motorcycle helmet; goggles; gloves; long pants; long-sleeved shirt; and over-the-ankle boots. Water and snacks are also a good idea. Check with the instructor to make sure your machine is appropriate for training. Children under 16 should never ride an adult ATV. Loaner machines may be available. Three wheelers are not allowed.

It is important that health care providers, citizens, and public officials work together to implement a comprehensive injury-prevention response to this serious health issue. —*Courtesy of the Oregon Department of Parks and Recreation*

22

The Road to Paradise—
McKenzie River Scenic Drive

When my boys were young, it seemed my family was destined to wander! We often unpacked our gear from one adventure, only to begin repacking a day or two later and then head down some other back road toward a new-to-us destination. In those days I gave my loved ones little choice really, but I think that's because the RV life made travel and adventure so easy. I enjoyed "getting away" for enjoyment and discovery across Oregon's varied and intriguing byways so much that I was often left wondering if we'd ever return home. But I will let you in on a secret: I'm not sure I had a choice—I should explain.

Many years ago, when the boys were very young—one in diapers, another just out, and the oldest son a mere first grader, a work assignment found me on a two-week tour along Alaska's famed Inside Passage. It was a rigorous schedule of 11 stops in 14 days that involved appointments, interviews, and travel via jet aircraft, floatplanes, helicopters, boats of varied sizes—even kayaks as we toured a Northwest paradise. Outdoor photographer Mark Plut called the trip a visit to "heaven on earth," for all the enchanting country that we explored from Prince Rupert to Anchorage. We produced a remarkable and highly popular ten-part series of stories and a 1-hour *Grant's Getaways* special television program. Yet as magical and unforgettable as the many adventures— and certainly the journey—were, the scene that

Belknap Bridge has been in continuous use since 1890.

was forever burned into my memory bank was the "Welcome Home" scene that occurred on my front porch when I returned home.

My wife, Chris McOmie, met me at the door and she was clearly tired and worn out as she held our two younger boys, Eric and Kevin—one per arm—while 6-year-old Grant stood at her side, his arms wrapped tightly around his mother's waist. She smiled—weakly—and said, "Ahhh, so glad you're home, dear! I have an idea—how about the next time you leave for a travel assignment that's measured by days, not hours—how 'bout we all go with you?" Her point was most certainly loving and well-intended but her message was also crystal clear: make more time for the family! So began a series of Oregon travel and adventure programs that came to be known as *Grant's Getaways: A Home on the Road* that allowed the kids to come along and join in on the fun of exploring and learning more about their home state as we traveled in a trailer or motor home RV.

One of our first adventures took us on a course for a patch of the Oregon Cascade Mountains that I'd not visited in many years. Our travel trailer was loaded to the gills as we meandered up the McKenzie River Valley on US 126, east of the Eugene-Springfield area. From its headwaters at Clear Lake, high in the Cascade Mountains, the McKenzie is a swift and lively river. The scenic drive explodes with opportunities to partake in outdoor activities amid some of Oregon's most beautiful mountain landscapes.

Our stops along this route included Goodpasture Bridge near Vida (45200 Goodpasture Road, Vida, OR 97488). At 165 feet in length, it is the second-longest covered bridge in Oregon. It's also where spring busts out all over with dramatic, colorful backdrops from every angle, so it's a great photo stop. A second and equally scenic covered bridge is the Belknap Bridge, located in the community of Rainbow (54498 McKenzie River Drive, Blue River, OR 97413). Stop the car and stretch your legs with a short hike around the Delta Old Growth Forest (located at Delta Campground, FS Road 400, McKenzie Bridge, OR 97413; 541-822-3381). The half-mile interpretive trail provides interesting insight into this fragile ecosystem and close-up views of 500-year-old trees nearly 250 feet (75 meters) tall.

If you like a campout, this is your byway, for there are many choices in many settings along the way. After a day of frenzied travel, our place to unwind is Paradise Campground. It truly is a wonder, one of fourteen US Forest Service (USFS) campgrounds within the McKenzie District of the Willamette National Forest. Paradise offers sixty-four campsites, and many of the sites are right along the stream, whether you stay in a tent or a motor home. Set in a classic Pacific Northwest semi–rain forest, Paradise Campground is cloaked in Douglas fir and hemlock trees. Rainfall is common throughout fall, winter, and spring, so do come prepared. The campground sits near the junction of Oregon 242 (leading to McKenzie Pass) and provides a convenient base camp from which to explore in many directions. River fishing (from nonmotorized boats) and picnicking are favorite pastimes here. A boat ramp, amphitheater, and restrooms are also available near the campground.

As you can imagine, the local folks take great pride in their corner of the Pacific Northwest. In fact, then US Forest Service Ranger Pam Navitsky told me, "We love the scenery, the history, and the quiet of this river—and we love to share its secrets with visitors. In fact, when you arrive, you quickly learn that the McKenzie River played a large role in Oregon's history as a lifeline for Native Americans, then trappers, then pioneer settlers, and now the locals." Today, the McKenzie River National Recreation Trail stretches along 25 miles of the banks of the river. With children in tow, choose part of the trail and explore it in smaller sections. Hikers and bikers should keep an eye out for each other, especially on narrow parts of the trail and on slopes. The trail is flat and easy to walk for the most part, with few climbs or switchbacks, and it is open to bicyclists, but trying to tackle the whole trail at once is challenging even for experienced bikers and hikers. McKenzie River Mountain Resort (541-822-6272) offers a shuttle service to help you plan a shorter hike or mountain bike adventure.

Whether hiking or driving along the river, you will encounter three scenic waterfalls—Sahalie, Koosah, and Tamolitch—that offer a nice break for relaxing a bit, plus each is spectacular enough for display in any Oregon calendar. After we pulled into the Sahalie Falls parking lot, my three sons raced from the car down the short and easy paved trail to an overlook that proved irresistible. We stood slack-jawed and spellbound for a half hour while admiring the plunge-pool falls dropping nearly a hundred feet. From Sahalie Falls, you can hike to nearby Koosah Falls, which drops about 70 feet top to bottom and is equally rewarding. (We were pleased that we carried our camera for a family photo, so don't forget yours.) The hike is a family-friendly 2.6-mile loop with a vault restroom at Sahalie Falls only. While the Sahalie Falls observation deck is wheelchair accessible, the trail between the falls is not. The closest trailhead to the pool is at Trail Bridge Reservoir off USFS Road 655. From the parking area at the trailhead, head east on the McKenzie River Trail for approximately 2 miles.

An equally splendid scenic drive begins at the junction of Oregon 126 and 242 and leads east to McKenzie Pass and beyond to Sisters, Oregon. This scenic drive follows an 1860s wagon route and crosses the Willamette and Deschutes

National Forests, first through Douglas fir, then ponderosa pine, and then stands of aspen. Scenic vistas along the byway provide beautiful views of the Three Sisters peaks as well as the surrounding wilderness.

When you reach 5,325-foot McKenzie Pass, you're surrounded by lava, so climb up to the nearby Dee Wright Observatory and savor the wide-screen panoramic view of six Cascades peaks. Dee Wright Observatory was named in honor of a Forest Service packer who served from 1910 to 1934 and was the foreman of the Civilian Conservation Corps crew that built the observatory. Nearby, enjoy the Lava River Trail, a half-mile loop and interpretive trail beginning at the observatory that winds through interesting lava gutters and crevasses. The parking area and observatory are all ADA accessible and restrooms are available. The paved trail is too, but note that steep grades and drop-offs can make it difficult for wheelchairs. Also use caution as the volcanic terrain can be hazardous. The basaltic lava here is rough and jagged; be sure to stay on marked trails.

Note: Oregon 242 is winding and narrow, so motor homes over 22 feet long and vehicles pulling trailers are discouraged from traveling. Depending upon snowfall, Oregon 242 is usually closed November to early July.

22A Paradise Campground

Where: From McKenzie Bridge, OR, travel 4 miles east on Highway 126 to the campground.
Web: fs.usda.gov; visitmckenzieriver.com/oregon/item/paradise-campground
Phone: 541-822-3381 (McKenzie River Ranger District); 877-444-6777 (reservations)

McKenzie River National Recreation Trail

Where: From McKenzie Bridge, OR travel 1 mile east on Highway 126 to the bottom trailhead.
Web: fs.usda.gov; mckenzierivertrail.com
Phone: 541-822-3381 (McKenzie River Ranger District)

22B Dee Wright Observatory

Where: From McKenzie Bridge, OR travel 5 miles east on Highway 126; take a right on Highway 242 and continue 22 miles to the observatory.
Web: fs.usda.gov
Phone: 541-822-3381 (McKenzie River Ranger District)

23

Digging into the Past—John Day Fossil Beds National Monument

The John Day Fossil Beds National Monument is a landscape of enormous vistas and endless horizons along one of the longest undammed rivers in the Lower 48. From its headwaters in the Blue Mountains to its salmon-rich confluence with the grand Columbia more than 225 miles away, the John Day River twists, turns, and carves a path through a 14,000-acre treasure trove of colorful volcanic history and some of the world's most important fossil beds. The national monument is a three-unit preserve that draws professionals and amateurs alike from many different fields—as well as the generally curious who want to learn more about Oregon's geologic history and a fossil record dating back 45 million years.

The Sheep Rock Unit (30 miles west of the town of John Day) is home to the monument's main visitor center and fossil collection. Colorful Sheep Rock looms above the narrow valley and its green fields on either side of the snaking river. That's about all the green you'll see at a place that turns time on its head. When you stare up at the brown and tan rock walls in the sweltering heat that cooks like an oven, it's hard to imagine that a lush, near-tropical forest once existed here. But according to the monument's curator and paleontologist, Josh Samuels, "the records in the rocks don't lie."

More than 300 fossilized plant species have been found in the Clarno Unit of the John Day Fossil Beds.

You need a strong arm, keen eyes, and plenty of patience to dig fossils for keeps at Wheeler High School.

Samuels added, "This is a wonderful area to study changes in plants and animals or biological evolution. We see animals coming into existence in these fossil beds and, millions of years later, disappearing. It's also an area where we have abundant fossils, so we go out and collect fossils there. It's a very important place."

Samuels said that visitors are best served to begin their adventures at the Thomas Condon Paleontology Center. The center is partially ADA accessible (lacks powered doors, open captioning, and wheelchair accessibility at information desk); there is no admission charge, but donations are always welcome. Samuels explained, "Condon started collecting fossils in the 1860s [he was actually a minister, so fossil collecting was a second job of sorts]. He found fossils in the area and sent them off to a variety of scientists at institutions in the country and really helped highlight what's been found in this area—brought it to the forefront of paleontology." The center has interactive and interpretive exhibits that will delight children of all ages including rocks and fossils that can be touched, a computer microscope to inspect them closely, and a viewing window to watch the paleontologists at work. Over 500 fossils are also on display to help explain both the geologic history of the area and the science of paleontology. And the area around the center has picnic facilities and trails to be explored. Samuels added that classes and lectures teach you more about the region, while the center's murals and fossils give perspective on periods that reach back 50 million years. "You really have a jungle in those times with things like crocodiles that truly contrast with today's dry, arid environment of open sagebrush and grassland environments with things like deer, mountain lions, and elk running around."

The center is administered by the National Park Service and also serves as an active research area, so you may chance upon the laboratory and see how specimens are prepared for analysis: the past is revealed in front of your eyes—one grain of rock and sand at a time. Technicians use patience and critical care to remove the rock to expose fossilized animals that lived so long ago. The Sheep Rock Unit is a good starting point for your journey through time. It prepares you to understand the remarkably vivid colors of the ash deposits at the Painted Hills Unit about 65 miles south of Sheep Rock and near Mitchell, Oregon.

The Painted Hills Unit lies at the end of a 3-mile paved access road. It's a popular site for photographers who wish to capture the brilliantly colored ash deposits that range from rose to pink, from gold to bronze, and seem splashed across the eroded contours of nearby hummocks and hills. This is the kind of treasure Oregon legends are made of, and I never tire of an early morning or late evening visit when the light is just peeking up or winking down the hillsides. Several short hiking trails allow closer inspection, and at the Painted Hills picnic area you will also find shaded picnic tables, water (May to September), and restrooms, as well as exhibits and trail guides.

At the Painted Cove Trail, you'll appreciate the fact that they have built a boardwalk above the environment in order to protect it—in this case, it's ash fall dating back 33 million years. Samuels noted, "It's a breathtaking view—we can actually see very colorful layers of rock—alternating bands of brown and red and some black. They really make it a photogenic place. The way the clay erodes gives it that beautiful color but also it's kind of a slow process, so any footprint will last for years—so if someone walks up on one of those hills we can see that for years so it's very important that people stay off the hills so we can preserve it for everyone."

"Leave no footprints and take only memories" is a standard and strict rule inside the parkland. Federal law protects all the natural and cultural resources in the John Day Fossil Beds National Monument and fossil collecting is strictly prohibited. Even researchers can collect only with a special permit and they must carry the permit with them at all times. So be sure not to disturb any treasures you may observe in the park.

The Clarno Unit sits 50 miles to the northwest on the banks of the John Day River. Here you'll witness a succession of ash-laden mudflows that repeatedly buried a forest landscape, leaving behind one of the finest fossilized collections of leaves, nuts, and seeds in North America—some 300 different species and counting. You may have the most fun up the road a piece at Wheeler High School in Fossil, Oregon, where you can dig the fossils—for keeps. Kids especially love that activity. Stroll through the back gate at the high school and pass under the goalposts to take up a handful of fossils that you can actually keep.

School Superintendent Brad Sperry told me, "It has been kind of a local secret, and the community knew about it, would come up and kick around in the rocks and pick up a fossil. Got on a couple websites and before long, it looks like today: busy." All you need to dig your own fossils are simple tools, a strong arm, keen eyes, curiosity, and a ton of patience. For just a few minutes, I dug, pried, and separated the layers of muddy shale and found perfectly preserved imprints of ferns, cedar fronds, and an unusual leaf. In less than an hour, I collected half a dozen very fine specimens to add to our family collection.

The specimens here date back more than 45 million years to when the local terrain was a rain forest and the larger area was home to huge pigs and enormous rhinos. Successive and massive mud and lava flows washed away or covered everything that stood in their way. Sperry explained, "None of these plants survived the era, of course, but it is the record of this tremendous diversity of life and the record of a totally catastrophic end that, taken together, really make you think."

Sperry noted that fossil digging isn't free—the district appreciates a donation of $5 per individual or $15 per family of four with $3 for each additional child. The donations support science and art education in this small rural school system. Sperry also emphasized that there's little need to take more than a handful of the fossils. He'd rather see more people coming back again and again instead of loading up by the bucketful. He said that simple tools, like a hammer and chisel—plus, a bucket—are all you need to get started. "It's all about kids and families and the excitement of finding fossils and realizing they're 30 million years old. It is like Christmas morning and seeing what Santa brought you. Well, take the rocks, crack them open, and suddenly it's Christmastime. You never know what you're going to find!"

Just down the street from the school, the Paleo Lands Institute will teach you much about the fossils that you collect and perhaps provide a new way to look at the high desert. Their visitor center hosts exhibits with interactive activities to help children and adults learn about the area. Free Wi-Fi and a charging station as well as coffee and tea are available. Call the institute to help you plan a day hike, photography hike, adventure trip, or cycling trip for your family while you're in the area.

Institute spokesperson Anne Mitchell said, "I think a lot of people come out and go, 'I want to dig up a fossil.' But when they actually get here, they start learning how it all goes together. This center was designed to be sort of a hands-on, get dirty and get comfortable with science and learn about fossils and geology."

"It really helps to present what people have right in their own backyards—there are fossils really," added Samuels. "These fossils are something that we can highlight and help others to appreciate the history of the area and the valuable natural resources that are here."

23A Thomas Condon Paleontology Center

Where: 32651 Highway 19, Kimberly, OR 97848
Web: nps.gov/joda
Phone: 541-987-2333

23B Wheeler High School in Fossil, Oregon

Where: 600 E B Street, Fossil, OR 97830
Web: oregonpaleolandscenter.com/wheeler-high-school-fossil-beds
Phone: 541-763-4303

Oregon Paleo Lands Institute

Where: 333 West Fourth Street, Fossil, OR 97830
Web: oregonpaleolandscenter.com
Phone: 541-763-4480

Watch the Episode: traveloregon.com/JohnDayFossils

24

Watching the Clouds Roll By— Cloud Cap Inn

As a child, a much-loved part of my Sunday afternoons was when my parents would bundle us youngsters up and shoo us out the door and into the family station wagon for a weekend country drive. It was natural for me to establish the same tradition when I became a father, and together my kids and I have had many wonderful times on the road from here to there, bound for no particular place and unburdened by cares. A favored excursion runs the little-traveled northern route toward Mt. Hood via Cloud Cap Road near Parkdale. This trail puts you face-to-face with a more dramatic side of Mt. Hood, and to borrow the phrase of a free US Forest Service brochure (available at an information kiosk along the route), "The mountains seem closer and the valleys deeper."

It is hard not to be drawn to Mt. Hood's rugged northern perspective marked by rocky crags, steep inclines, and the gigantic Eliot Glacier. On the way to the mountain, I am drawn to the many family-owned farms and orchards of the Hood River Valley. Each September, the trees bear the heavy weight from an early fruit bounty. Farms like Kiyokawa Family Orchards near Parkdale, Oregon, will entice you with an incredible variety of apples and pears. In addition to their beautiful view of Mt. Hood and a fruit stand featuring pies, turnovers, honey, jams, and cider, the orchard has beautiful grounds for picnicking and a play area for kids. And bring your own bags or boxes to take advantage of the opportunity to pick your own fruit. Owner Randy Kiyokawa said that visitors enjoy their 3 acres of "you-pick" fruit: "No ladders are required, so it's really a lot of fun whether you're two and a half to six feet tall—there will be an apple there for you to pick!"

Another delicious moment waits for you at the Apple Valley Country Store

The northern approach to Mt. Hood is steep and rugged.

where they whip up some of the thickest milkshakes around according to owner Bob White: "We take a scoop of fresh huckleberries, mix it with some of our huckleberry jam for a bit of sweetness, and then mix it with three scoops of Tillamook ice cream and blend it up and you'll be amazed!" They also sell over fifty jams, jellies, and syrups that they make in their own canning kitchen and have a spacious picnic area with plenty of room for the kids to stretch their legs. It's a place that stays in touch with history too—reaching back a century when hardware, antiques—even fishing tackle—ruled the scene! It's a fine warm-up for the history lesson that waits just up the road on the route toward Mt. Hood via Cloud Cap.

It's a drive offering exceptional views—especially at Inspiration Point, where on a cloudless day you can gaze from the small parking area across to Wallalute Falls and Mt. Hood. The high elevation (5,000 feet) is noteworthy, too, for the air seems cleaner and the views sharper as you round each bend on this rough roadway. The fir and hemlock part every now and then to reveal spectacular forest scenery. Take note of the trees throughout these sites. Forest rangers have told me that tree-ring samples taken from this part of the forest indicate volcanic ash is present here and dates to approximately 1800—a clear indication of Mt. Hood's eruptive past. This will feel like a real adventure for the kids, especially as the road changes from pavement to rock and gravel and includes 9 miles of rutted and steep dirt road with many potholes. It is not for the faint of heart, so be prepared for some bumps along the way unless you drive a vehicle with 2 feet of ground clearance.

The welcome mat is always out for visitors interested in a unique chapter of

Established in 1926, the Hood River Crag Rats are the oldest mountain rescue group in the nation. Photo courtesy of the Crag Rats.

Oregon history at the Cloud Cap Inn. Built in 1889, it was actually the very first hotel on Mt. Hood. In fact, folks came from all over the world to make the 2-day trip to get up this side of the mountain for the alpine scenery. But distance and transportation—plus tough economic times, made the Cloud Cap Inn an uncertain business operation, and its run as a mountain hostelry ended after 35 years.

In fact, with the start of WWII people's interest in alpine vacations disappeared entirely as interest in the home front war defense effort rose. So much so that by 1950, the Forest Service was talking of demolishing Cloud Cap because of vandalism and the effects of the weather. That's when the Crag Rats took over! The Hood River, Oregon, based search and rescue team took responsibility for Cloud Cap Inn in 1954 and saved it from demolition.

Longtime Crag Rats Bernie Wells and Bill Pattison agreed that the Cloud Cap Inn makes visitors feel right at home "This is the most dramatic side of the mountain," noted Pattison. "There's the Cooper Spur Trail and climbing route—there's massive Eliot Glacier with incredible geologic formations—plus the quiet alpine setting of trees and wildflowers. Such a different world from the Timberline [southern] point of view, and it just gets into your heart." At the oldest alpine mountain lodge in the West, the site feels more like a museum than a base of operations for search and rescue. Bernie Wells is happy to show visitors around and pleased to show off the valuable restoration effort that has given the old inn new life.

"It got to the point where we realized we could not keep up with the deterioration," said Wells. "So we put into effect a long-term restoration project that lasted for 12 years. We were able to go through the entire building and restore it back to the way it was." They certainly gave Cloud Cap's old bones a new life, but they also held on to important history too—like the "signature wall" that's located in one of the seven bunkrooms.

"As people came up to stay on the mountain, they would write on this wall who they were with at the time—some of these signatures are from the 1800s." Wells added it's even more remarkable—given the many fires that roared across the forest and even right over Cloud Cap Inn—that the building still stands. "Most wooden buildings constructed like this have burned from open food fires and the like—we've come close over 120 years—but thankfully, it's still here."

Thanks to the US Forest Service and the 105 members of the Crag Rats, Cloud Cap Inn is open to visitors who admire the view and the inn's connection with Oregon's past. If you'd like to visit and tour Cloud Cap Inn, the US Forest Service offers free guided tours each Sunday during the summer. Tours generally start at 11:00 A.M. and at 1:00 P.M. and last approximately 45 minutes to 1 hour.

The tours are limited to twelve people per group. Reservation slots go quickly, so book your tour early. The reservation system protects the inn and ensures visitors get a quality historical experience.

24A Kiyokawa Family Orchards

Where: 8129 Clear Creek Road, Parkdale, OR 97041
Web: kiyokawafamilyorchards.com
Phone: 541-352-7115

24B Apple Valley Country Store

Where: 2363 Tucker Road, Hood River, OR 97031
Web: applevalleystore.com
Phone: 541-386-1971

24C Cloud Cap Inn

Where: Cloud Cap Road, Mt. Hood, OR 97041
Web: cragrats.org/cloudcap (for tour information search "Cloud Cap Inn Tours" at fs.usda.gov)
Phone: 541-352-6002 (Hood River Ranger Station)

Watch the Episode: traveloregon.com/FruitLoopCloudCap

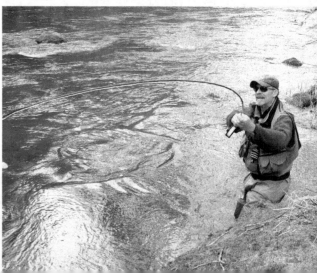

Grant McOmie's Outdoor Talk— Oregon's Fish Whisperer

This story is for every parent who has wondered whether their actions—big or small, filled with prideful intent or simply by accident—make a difference, any sort of difference—to the pathway their kids choose in life. If you ask Jay Nicholas, he will tell you how his dad made a difference that helped him find his life's passion for the out-of-doors.

Jay Nicholas is Oregon's former "salmon czar" and more than 20 years ago, he led the effort to save the state's wild coastal salmon. His passion for Oregon's salmon and steelhead is measured by the numerous books that he has written, his drawings and paintings, plus, the artistic touch he brings to his hand-tied salmon flies. He knows the habits of salmon so well that many have nicknamed Nicholas "Oregon's fish whisperer."

"People ask me, what's the most effective pattern? Well, the best fly is the one I caught my last fish on, the second best pattern is the previous fly that I caught a fish on, and then the third best is the fly I haven't tied yet," noted the longtime fisherman with a chuckle.

Nicholas ties flies that drive fish wild and he is one of Oregon's best. Nicholas credits his undying passion for all things fishy to a childhood that was rich with opportunities when he joined his dad. "I was probably 5 and Dad went fishing on a stream where I *saw* a fish for the first time in my

Jay Nicholas credits his father for his fishing passion and love for all things outdoors.

life and I was captivated by it. Learning to fish in Oregon was stirred by that experience and by the time I was 13, I had cast lines into the Metolius River, Olallie Lake, and Round Lake near Mt. Hood, and it was my father who gave me the chance."

Nicholas was also fortunate to cross paths with a fly-tying legend in Portland's Meier and Frank store—he visited the sporting goods department every chance he could to watch and learn from Audrey Joy. "I grew up in Portland and my most lasting and positive memory was going to the downtown Meier and Frank store and watching a lady named Audrey Joy tie flies. She had a little cubicle in the sporting goods department and there I was—just a kid and fascinated by her work. I often wonder how many kids learned to tie flies watching Audrey Joy."

She was born in Idaho and as a teen began tying flies for her father, John Joy, who invented a sewing machine that could speed up the fly-tying process. Audrey arrived in Portland in the '40s after WWII and found a position at the Meier and Frank store. For more than 20 years, she tied at her sewing machine an estimated 300,000 flies and her little booth became a shrine for youngsters and adults alike. Nicholas added, "One of the things I remember about Audrey was she had her fly-tying vise hooked up to an old treadle-type sewing machine. She had the thing rigged so she could turn whatever fly she had in her vise by simply applying foot pressure on the sewing machine treadle."

Nicholas was hooked and soon began tying flies and even selling them to other fly fishermen "I tied some parachute flies and began selling them and with my money I bought a fly rod, reel, line, and a box of a dozen leaders and then I went fishing. . . . I remember everything about it."

Nicholas explained that tying flies requires learning varied techniques that require special skills just like a painter or a sculptor who works with clay. It's a tactile effort that requires an eye for the materials and how to move them into just the right position to match an insect's appearance. "It's all about hand-eye coordination! As I feel the materials, I imagine how they will refract the water; plus, how the fly will rise and drop as I retrieve through the water—but I always wonder—do the fish really care?"

A puzzling question from the man once considered Oregon's salmon czar: back in 1997, Nicholas was lead scientist and author of a landmark conservation plan to save wild coastal salmon from extinction—it was called the Oregon Plan. "I worked with farmers, loggers, fishermen, pro-hatchery, anti-hatchery people, and the vision of the Oregon Plan was that all the state agencies would authentically incorporate the health of salmon into their missions—and they have—to a point."

Nicholas said he grew weary of "fish politics" and 4 years ago he decided it was time for a change and so he simply "went fishing." That's when he turned his interest in fish science to fly tying and book writing and art. "My favorite subjects are salmon and flies that catch them. As my fishing interests have expanded, I've been drawing albacore tuna, sea bass, and lingcod—if you look closely in the mouth of a ling, my gosh, talk about a toothy critter."

In a search for the humanity in angling, Oregon's fish whisperer has discovered much more: it *isn't* the "catch" that matters the most—but what we might catch when we go to Oregon's waters. "We're a bunch of fishermen," said Nicholas. "We usually just talk guy talk, but 2 percent of the time—and not with everyone —you get to share the really important stuff in life . . . and I think that's what it's all about."

Nicholas has written eleven books on the nitty-gritty tactics and techniques to catch fish with a fly—all published within a year—he said he's on a "mad dash" to write and publish more books about fish and fishing too! "When I find myself awake at 3:30 in the morning and I can't sleep and I can't fish, I write—so I guess you could call me a driven man." That—plus the fact he has survived two heart attacks and now has five stents in his chest. "My cardiologist said, 'Jay—you're fine and you're going to be fine until you're not.' So I don't worry about it—I just get on with it."

And he has—he said that of the books he's written, one of his favorites is called *Home Waters*—a short 20-minute read of poetry and homage to Oregon's salmon and steelhead anglers:

"We talk while we fish—man-talk usually—we talk of flies, fly lines, and our hooks. Sometimes though, we share more intimate thoughts . . . hope and fear, failure and triumph, our sons and daughters, mothers and fathers, war, the passing of friends, the certainty of our own death, obsession and depression, rage, passion, courage, God, women—probably there is too little such talk among men."

When asked about the most profound influences in his life, Nicholas remembers his boyhood adventures and prizes those memories above all. He insisted that his youthful days outdoors were launching points for a career that's taken him to many distant places and in many unexpected directions. "As I was growing up, I was just as excited about hooking 5-inch shiners [perch] as a little boy," he recalled. Today, while he'll fish with any method at hand, he packs his fly gear on every trip, just in case—he has a rod and weight-tailored line for every offshore rockfish, lingcod, albacore, etc.

In his heart, Nicholas believes that his love for fishing and for all things outdoors is founded in the "doing of the thing" when his father gave him the chance, so Nicholas's lasting memories are of casting worms or hand-tied flies into small ponds and narrow Oregon streams. He caught his first chinook salmon on a fly from the Rogue River and immediately sold all his other tackle. "It's like a handshake from God, only it's deeper, it's more powerful and bigger than I can explain. I remember everything about it and I am thankful that my father gave me the chance to do it."

25

Ticket2Ride

When you have a "Ticket2Ride," there's no telling how far you can travel! Twenty-six fifth-grade students from Southeast Portland's Marysville Elementary School recently gathered for science class along the Maple Ridge Trail at Tryon Creek State Park in Lake Oswego. Their field trip teacher for the day was Julie Baweja, a science expert from ECO, or Ecology Classrooms Outdoors (ecologyoutdoors.org), who said that youngsters are always eager learners: "It is oftentimes the first time they've been outside of their school in a huge park setting like Tryon Creek—that's amazing and fun to just get them out and excited."

Tryon Creek State Natural Area is a wonderful spot to visit with children and is only about 15 minutes from downtown Portland. The park offers 8 miles of hiking trails, 3½ miles of horse trails, a 3-mile paved bike trail, and a paved accessible trail that can be perused on your own, but regularly scheduled, free guided hikes and nature classes are also available for nature lovers of all ages. Several times a week Tryon Creek hosts a Preschool Story and Stroll for families with children ages 2 to 6 (though all ages are welcome). No reservation is required, but space is allotted on a first come, first served basis, so arrive about a half hour before the class begins. The 75-minute class incorporates art, literature, movement, and outdoor play with nature exploration. Open daily, the nature center has exhibits, a store, and restrooms, and frequently hosts themed educational open houses and special events.

On this day, the class visiting Tryon Creek was part of the Ticket2Ride program that enables K-8 schools in minority and low- to moderate-income communities to use Oregon's state parks for experiential learning, a sort of outdoor science lab (oregonstateparksfoundation.org/ticket-2-ride). "We know that children have a natural curiosity," said Gwen Van Doosselaere, the director of ECO. "They come outside and everything is new and everything sparkles and they can run around. It engages all of their senses and it's a very embodied experience."

It's a unique blend of hands-on environmental education with the generous support from the nonprofit Oregon State Parks Foundation that makes the experience happen. Oregon State Parks already supports learning for hundreds of schools each year. They have accessible and inspiring locations, experienced, dedicated staff, and offer inspirational and effective learning experiences. The schools simply need to be able to get the kids to the parks.

Tryon Creek State Park is a magical place with many trails to explore.

"When I found out that many urban kids were being forced to stay in their schools and work with their computers and books and can't get outside to touch the leaves and learn about the animals and the rocks and trees, I said, 'I want to do something about that,'" said Seth Miller, the director of the Oregon State Parks Foundation. "Our parks are natural classrooms bursting with opportunity for students to capture their fascination with science, if we can just get them outdoors!"

Once in the parks, a world of learning begins as young people discover their natural, cultural, and historical heritage and enjoy recreational opportunities.

"These experiences can set kids on a trajectory to a lifelong fascination with, and participation in, numerous areas of biological, chemical, physical, and earth sciences, and begin a lifelong relationship with the great outdoors," added Miller.

The foundation pays for bus transportation to get the kids to the parks. The park even supplies rangers like Deb Hill, who showed off the bones and skulls of varied wildlife species and talked about their natural history: "We have more than 260 parks in a world-class state park system," said Hill. "We have beaches, rivers, mountains, canyons, forests, waterfalls, volcanoes, and fields all available as outdoors science labs! Tryon Creek State Park is a magical park—it can feel like you are out in wilderness down by the creek. You don't hear the traffic and it can almost feel like you're out in the wilderness. It's a tremendous place to learn."

The sheer variety of ECO lessons is remarkable; from fish, trees, moss, and lichens to guided tours on plant identifications, rain forest tours, and even history tours.

"Many of our parks also offer great history lessons," said Miller. "Opportunities to learn about lumber, agriculture, the Oregon Trail, the Civilian Conservation Corps. Oregon State Parks can enhance learning for hundreds of schools each year."

In the event that elementary school teachers are not prepared to teach the in-class science lessons, Ticket2Ride connects with the nonprofit ECO to support the experiential park lessons with three pre-visit and three post-visit lessons to the classroom. In fact, the Marysville student's classroom teacher, Kelli Joy, noted that ECO made learning fun: "I look forward to their lessons as much as the students do! It's such a treat to get these students out into nature, and experiencing it first-hand is making them better stewards."

So far, during the fall of 2016, nine Portland schools have participated in Ticket2Ride. The Oregon State Parks Foundation is encouraged and eager to make the program grow bigger. "The greater vision is to open this program up statewide to any school in Oregon," said Ward Johnson, Ticket2Ride program manager. "The purpose would be to fund the transportation—often it's that transportation that's the hardest thing to getting kids out to the parks."

"Children are spending less time than ever before in the great outdoors," said Miller. "Television, video games, homework, computers, the internet, busy families, and strained budgets all conspire to reduce our children's exposure to nature." In fact, sedentary activities are linked with the rise in childhood obesity. According to the Centers for Disease Control, childhood obesity has more than doubled in children and quadrupled in adolescents in the past 30 years. Increasing evidence demonstrates the many benefits of nature on children's psychological and physical well-being, including reduced stress, greater physical health, more creativity, and improved concentration. Gwen Van Doosselaere summed it up well: "For a lot of these kids, Ticket2Ride can end up shaping—really, the rest of their lives."

---

25 Tryon Creek State Natural Area

Where: 11321 SW Terwilliger Boulevard, Portland, OR 97219

Web: oregonstateparks.org; tryonfriends.org

Phone: 503-636-9886; 800-551-6949

Watch the Episode: traveloregon.com/Ticket2Ride

26

Secrets in the Sand—
Float Fairies

In October, except for the surf and wind, the pace of life along the Oregon coastline slows down. Long gone are the jam-packed summer vacation days when the tourist traffic on US 101 speeds by at a shattering pace. Nor are the campgrounds filled with youngsters' raucous, rowdy chorus under a shimmering sun. Those days are on hold—at least for another 6 months or so—and there's a very powerful and practical reason for this fact: Fall and winter storms can be downright nasty, scary affairs! They tease you, dare you, and then lash at you in the secluded warmth of your vehicle as you prepare for a beach stroll. Then they descend upon you with a blast that jostles and rattles and shakes your car from side

Glass floats are treasures that you can find on Lincoln City beaches.

to side. That's before the pelting rain begins—the stuff that pops and explodes across the hood and windshield and then wraps its watery arms completely around you.

No doubt about it, storm watching on the coast is a chilling proposition, but let's also be clear that it can be addicting fun! In fact, there's a growing crowd of storm watchers who thrive in this seasonal mayhem, folks who love to visit the coast when the weather's at its worst. They know there's a breathtaking reward between the storms, especially during a stroll along the more than 7 miles of sandy shoreline at Lincoln City. As I discovered, fall can be the best time to

At the Jennifer Sears Glass Art Studio in Lincoln City, you can create your own gorgeous glass floats.

chance upon unique and artistic treasures in the form of beautiful glass floats that have been "seeded" on the beach for you to find. This is a great way to spend an exciting afternoon with your children at the Oregon coast. Along the sand with their eyes scanning immediately to the left and then to the right and then in front of them—back and forth they go—they're beachcombers and they're having a blast. Why not? When you have a chance to find a shiny shell, an unusual rock, or a unique piece of distorted driftwood, who doesn't relish the idea of seeking treasures from the tides?

In the Lincoln City area, folks may cross paths with local resident Wayne Johnson—a self-proclaimed "float wizard" who makes certain that beachcombers have something special to find. "The fact is it's kind of undercover work that I do. First, it's hidden and I try not to be seen by anyone. And then I hide something colorful and prized too. I like that part of it a lot." Like a secret agent, Johnson stealthily moved among sea-strewn logs and lush beach grass to hide beautiful, colorful glass floats. Johnson said that he and a dozen other float wizards hide up to seventy glass floats along 7.5 miles of Lincoln City beaches beginning each week from October through May. "We want them visible and yet hidden enough so that it will be difficult for anyone to see them at first glance—we want it to be a challenge to find them."

Johnson explained to me that decades ago the storms would often deposit

Japanese glass fishing floats, softball-sized greenish globes that had floated for thousands of miles over many years across the Pacific Ocean, where they would finally go ashore on Oregon's beaches. As fishermen converted to plastic floats, the flow of glass floats virtually ended—until 1999, when the first Glass Float Odyssey was born. Originally designed by local artist Bryan Duncan, Lincoln City's inaugural glass float event was a hit and it is now an annual winter event. Lincoln City has many public beach access points, but when visiting with children, it's especially useful to know that NW 26th Street and NW 15th Street have restrooms available. Along the windswept shoreline near the mouth of the Siletz River, Johnson explained it's the anticipation of finding a special treasure that intrigues so many visitors. "It is really fun to come down here and actually find something that you can take home with you, say driftwood or agates or shells. I look for places among the logs or little clumps of grass. Sometimes, if there's an open sandy area, I'll just drop one down." He sheepishly grinned and added, "Walk, walk, and walk—the only way you're going to find them."

Well, that's not entirely true, for each of the exquisitely colored 8-inch globes is autographed and numbered by one of the area's local glass artists. So if you'd rather not search for treasure on the beach itself visit the nearby Jennifer Sears Glass Art Studio in Lincoln City. You can see the challenge that it takes to create a glass float—in fact, you can even learn how to do it yourself—with the help of local artists like Kelly Howard. She noted, "People always say, 'Anyone can watch the glassblower but we never get to try it.' Well, here is the chance to do just that. Try it, you may get hooked on it." Participation in the glassblowing process is open to adults and children over the age of 8. While the studio is open every day, you can make your own glass Wednesdays through Sundays but make a reservation ahead of time. Remember you're dealing with superheated elements, so closed-toe shoes are essential and the studio advises against wearing fleece fabrics. The cooling process requires that your project stays at the studio overnight, so you can pick it up the following day or have it shipped to you. Glassblowing is one of those activities that may leave a huge smile on your face just like it did for my youngest son, Kevin McOmie. He joined me on a recent coastal adventure and he was anxious to try his hands at glassblowing. Kevin, an accomplished art student who specializes in painting and drawing, had never tried anything like glass art before. But he soon got the knack of it and with Howard's patient demeanor and easy-to-follow instructions —he was deeply into the art of glass within 15 minutes.

First, Howard pulled a glob of molten glass from the 2,100-degree furnace. The material glowed yellow and red-hot from the heat. She showed Kevin how to roll it and then apply color with other small pieces of glass. "OK, Kevin, just blow and we'll expand the glass into a float—look! That's amazing isn't it, you're doing great." Howard coached as Kevin blew into a long rubber hose attached to the end of a 5-foot-long hollow rod. The glass globe at the other end magically grew into a fiery float. Kevin noted, "It really is fun! But you have to keep an eye on it—it's using a lot of skills all at once. In the end, I think I've created something really awesome that I'm going to remember for a long time."

The Jennifer Sears Studio is one of several glass art houses in the central Oregon coast area that's participating in the glass float project. Each float is like a moment of fiery magic that's captured in a heartbeat and leaves you spellbound. Howard added, "To see something get made and then realize that you had a hand in creating it, especially something made out of glass—well, it really is mesmerizing and different."

Back on the beach, Wayne Johnson insisted that the adventure of creating your own glass float or finding one that the float wizards hide on the sand is a difference that anyone will enjoy. "When you see it lying on the beach, it's kind of like finding beach treasure . . . something special on the Oregon coast." As I hiked alongside and watched Johnson hide a half-dozen floats, he offered a helpful tip for visitors: "I'll be out on the beach hiding these floats during the day, between the high tide line and the base of the cliff. We're not putting them anywhere you'd have to climb up, so look in dips in the sand or around logs, even in small piles of seaweed that have washed ashore." Such useful advice will help you turn a treasure hunt into a getaway memory of discovery along the coast.

26A Lincoln City Beaches

Where: Lincoln City, OR 97367
Web: lincolncity.org
Phone: 541-996-1274 (Visitor and Convention Bureau)

Jennifer Sears Glass Art Studio

Where: 4821 SW Highway 101, Lincoln City, OR 97367
Web: jennifersearsglassart.com
Phone: 541-996-2569

Watch the Episode: traveloregon.com/sandsecrets

Oregon Cannons Come Home

The late Rich Mulcahy liked to say, "There's something about treasure hunting that's irresistible and compelling, especially when it touches Oregon history and offers unique outdoor adventures too. I think it's that I am going after something that's been lost and I am digging in the sand to find it. I love to dig stuff."

Mulcahy walked long, lonely stretches of the Oregon coast each day accompanied only by the excited sounds of his handheld metal detector; the device was his constant companion. He swept the sand with the detector and marked each spot where something's hidden just below the surface. Most days, Mulcahy said he would discover common everyday objects on his adventures but he was intrigued by rediscovering history in the beach's sandy layers. Many of his so-called targets were easy to recognize once he had them in hand—they ranged from silver coins to gold wedding rings and other metallic jewelry.

But every now and then he found real head-scratchers, like his exotic Chinese copper coins and even a Roman coin that dates back nearly 2,000 years.

"Well, I shouldn't be surprised given the number of shipwrecks that we've had off the Oregon coast," explained Mulcahy. "I'm sure that there's material from those old wrecks that have come in with the tide." As long as mariners have traveled the ocean, ships have wandered too close to shore and been caught by powerful storms. They've also been guided by a captain's poor judgment so the ship and crew often ended in disaster on the beach.

Every now and then the tides and time reveal something unexpected— not measured by the value of gold or silver—but the chance to connect with rich Oregon history—like the two small cannons, or carronades, that were found at Arch Cape beach in 2008. A dad and daughter—Miranda Petrone and Michael Petrone—were strolling the shoreline when she saw something inside a thick coating of sand and rock; it was something nearly impossible to discern but it was Oregon history!

Experts believed they were two guns that came from the USS *Shark,* a navy schooner that shipwrecked on the Columbia River Bar in 1846. The two cannons and a chunk of the deck floated south and then washed ashore—only to be buried on the beach for 162 years. Staff from the Oregon Parks and Recreation Department (OPRD) recovered the two cannons and then shipped them to Texas A&M University's Marine Conservation Lab in 2009. OPRD paid $45,000 for the cannon restoration project.

Five years later, the Oregon cannons came home and the restoration is remarkable, the cannons are exceptional, and Astoria's Columbia River Maritime Museum is their new, permanent home. "They look new essentially," said Dave Pearson, the museum's administrator. "You would never believe that these were the carronades that were buried in the sand for 162 years." Behind the scenes, the Maritime Museum's curator, Jeff Smith, showed off scores of other pieces from the cannons—including an original oak platform, plus wrought iron fasteners, pins, rings, and leather coverings that secured one of the 18-pound guns.

And then there's one particularly puzzling, large ball of twine. "This was down inside the gun with this frayed twine material hanging out," said Smith. "A wooden plug was shoved in the end of the barrel to keep it dry and prevent rust or deterioration from the sea spray. In fact, when we first found the cannon and saw that, we wondered: could the cannon be loaded?"

Fortunately, it wasn't! But what was found is an amazing chapter of Oregon history—that connects with a time when the US Navy waved the American flag to the British who had long staked a claim to the Northwest region. Smith said the restored guns link us to an important moment for Oregonians. "If these elements had not survived, we probably wouldn't care that much about the USS Shark. But in 1846, Oregon was still an area that was disputed—was Oregon to be British or American? I think the Oregon question was answered with the mission of the USS Shark."

The Columbia River Maritime Museum is open daily and children age 5 and younger are admitted free. Exhibits are appropriate for all ages and are reflective of the history, nature, and culture of the area. You can also take a tour of a floating lighthouse (the lightship *Columbia*) or watch a 3D movie. Special events and classes are held throughout the year. Allow 2 hours for your visit to take in all the exhibits.

26B Columbia River Maritime Museum

Where: 1792 Marine Drive, Astoria, OR 97103
Web: crmm.org
Phone: 503-325-2323
Watch the Episode: TravelOregon.com/Cannons

27

Oregon Hoodoos

W hat is it about Oregon's rivers—they simply fascinate us: they offer cool, restful moments along their shady shorelines—but there's more if you know where to look. That's especially true near Camp Sherman where the Metolius River bubbles from the ground to curl and wind along an 8,600-acre river corridor. It is so special a place that it's been protected as one of America's Wild and Scenic Rivers since 1988.

Jeff Perin, a local fishing guide and the owner of The Fly Fishers Place in nearby Sisters, likes it that way. Perin often goes to the Metolius River near Wizard Falls, a rough-and-tumble stretch broken by moments of calm water: "You don't have spring creeks like this in too many places where the water just bubbles out of the ground at 45 degrees. It is such a special place."

It is so special a place that the Oregon Department of Fish and Wildlife (ODFW) has operated the nearby Wizard Falls Hatchery since 1947. Steve Hamburger, retired ODFW hatchery manager, said the cold water is the reason; it's the perfect water for raising trout. More than 4 million baby trout are raised at Wizard Falls Hatchery for release into scores of lakes and ponds across Oregon. Visitors come from all over the state too and stroll the 35-acre hatchery grounds that are more akin to a parkland than a fish hatchery. If you arrive when the hatchery is open, friendly

Youngsters can lend a hand feeding trout at Wizard Falls Hatchery.

This nest of Oregon hoodoos seems to stand guard over the Metolius Arm of Lake Billy Chinook.

staff will gladly explain the hatchery process to you. Otherwise, interpretive signs are located around the grounds for a self-guided tour. Bring some quarters to buy a handful of food and your kids can feed the growing fish. You can even hike along the Metolius here too. Picnic areas and restrooms are available at the hatchery.

Nearby campgrounds make the living easy too. There are ten US Forest Service Campgrounds along the Metolius River that offer a place to stay and relax—like Allen Springs Campground (recreation.gov). There are no hookups, phones, or TV at these campgrounds; it's self-contained camping without fancy conveniences, but Hamburger said that's OK for the returning campers: "They came here when they were kids and now they have kids, so bringing their youngsters out carries on from generation to generation. They really do enjoy that and the kids love it."

Jeff Perin added, "It's so beautiful here and we have so much great water—at any given time in Central Oregon, there's always some place to go." But in September of 2003, people wanted to go anywhere but here when two major forest fires merged into a catastrophic blaze called the B&B Complex Fires. More than 2,300 firefighters battled the B&B for 34 days at a cost pegged at $38 million. The huge blaze burned more than 90,00 acres along the crest of the Cascades near Mt. Jefferson.

Today, you can travel the back roads where pavement turns to gravel and explore the scorched landscape above the Metolius Arm of Lake Billy Chinook. Here, the B&B burned everything down to bare soil, but it also revealed something unusual most folks had never seen: the Oregon hoodoos. On a day when the wind really kicked up, the Metolius River ghost rocks—or balancing rocks—actually own a history that goes way back to 1855 when a Pacific Railroad survey crew came through this country looking for a faster way from California to the Columbia River. A US Army Lieutenant, one H. L. Abbot, coined the very first phrase describing the unique rock formations—he called them the "Oregon hoodoos."

The nest of unique rock pedestals—some thirty of them—are the hardened capstones of an ancient lava flow and an interesting sight for any young nature or rock lover in your family. As the softer material erodes beneath the basalt rock, the pillars that support the caps can grow up to 25 feet tall. While some hoodoos have tumbled down to the ground, geologists say the hoodoo formation process takes up to 20,000 years. It's a lonesome land where Oregon's hoodoos stand guard—but it is worth your time for a visit to see one of Oregon's stranger scenic areas. To find the hoodoos, drive to Madras, Oregon, then to Culver, 2½ hours from Portland. Drive west through Cove Palisades State Park, as though bound for Perry South campground in the Deschutes National Forest. Look for the Oregon Hoodoos parking area and trailhead 12.2 miles west of the Deschutes River arm bridge (this is 0.3 mile beyond where the road switches from pavement to gravel).

27 Wizard Falls Hatchery

Where: 7500 Forest Service Road 14, Camp Sherman, OR 97730
Web: dfw.state.or.us
Phone: 541-595-6611
Watch the Episode: traveloregon.com/Hoodoos

28

Taking Aim at Archery

John Strunk dreams of carving the perfect bow from the perfect piece of wood. He gently draws a knife blade across the bark of a vine maple stick and paper-thin curlicue strips of shaved maple rise, fall, and float to the floor. As Strunk carefully crafts his next "tool" from the 6-foot long, lanky stick of wood, it's clear that the Tillamook County resident has a master bow maker's touch. "When I start cutting out a bow, my hunt, my thoughts, my dreams are all generating at the same time," said Strunk. He added, "If you really try you can build a bow just like the Native Americans."

For nearly 40 years, Strunk has tried and succeeded in creating everything he needs just like native people might have: the bows, the arrows, quivers, and broadheads. The natural materials he prefers for bow making include bamboo, maple, osage, and the long popular and gorgeous yew wood: "Yew is probably one of the most used woods in archery in the northern hemisphere," he said with a smile.

The native Oregonian said his passion for the bow was born as a kid—watching movies like *Robin Hood* that starred the then-popular Hollywood actor Errol Flynn. "I love to shoot a bow just to see an arrow fly and it gives me more pleasure to do it with a bow that I have made," declared Strunk. He's a longtime hunter who is among the best in the country at building bows in a form called traditional or primitive archery.

The retired Tillamook schoolteacher not only excels at building the bows and arrows, but at shooting with them too. He admitted that an evening doesn't go by after he leaves the shop behind that he doesn't step into the backyard to shoot

John Strunk's passion for building bows began when he was a child and saw the movie Robin Hood.

arrows. "You need to train the muscles that are needed for shooting and that is done only by shooting lots of arrows. To me, that's the essential love affair that I have with this sport. If I'm not using what I create then I lose interest in it."

If you spend a day with Shawn Woods, the manager of the E. E. Wilson Wildlife Area near Corvallis, you will learn many ancient survival skills, like finding the right shaft of wood in the wild to make an arrow. Woods is a wilderness skills expert who admires the ancient ways of archery—starting with arrows made of a native rose called *Nootka*. "Especially when they grow in tight clumps. They try to get more sunlight and make these really tight shoots that are long and slim and perfect for arrow making—this is just like the traditional way—the way Native Americans would do it."

Woods's tool of choice for cutting the rose branch is as old as the Oregon story: a sharp block of obsidian. Obsidian is a volcanic glass found in Central Oregon and it's been used for cutting blades, spear points, and arrowheads for thousands of years. "We're really fortunate in Oregon to have obsidian for it only occurs in places that have volcanic geologic history. It's so much sharper than any metal," noted Woods. He added that obsidian edges are 200 times sharper than a stainless steel surgical scalpel. "It's really sharp and a beautiful piece of rock," added Woods. "It makes a great arrowhead and I used an antler to help shape it in a process called flint napping." He learned these skills—like flint napping obsidian with deer antler—the hard way—by trial and error! Woods said his success at arrow making isn't measured by the amount of time it takes to make just the right

Archers Afield in Tigard, Oregon, is a fine place for youngsters to learn how to use a bow and arrow.

arrowhead, but the pounds of rock he's broken in the process. "Fun to make 'em, that's for sure, but it is a tedious process too," he said with a chuckle.

Woods is in a good position to share his knowledge and his passion for archery. E. E. Wilson Wildlife Area is the site of the Oregon Department of Fish and Wildlife (ODFW)'s new covered archery range—it is open every day to anyone, any age—for free, though you need a wildlife area parking permit, which you can purchase online (dfw.state.or.us/conservationstrategy/parking.asp) and print at home because passes are not available at the wildlife area. You can visit the range during one of the many instructional times when loaner equipment is available (odfwcalendar.com) or at other times bring your own archery equipment. A covered area for archers makes this a year-round opportunity. Woods said there has been a recreation resurgence in a sport that's as old as human culture, where all you need is a stick, a piece of string, and a shaft of wood to discover that the world of archery is alive and well in Oregon. In fact, an ODFW Area is making archery easier for people to access.

Volunteers like Carl Swartz, past president of the Oregon Bow Hunters organization (oregonbowhunters.com) helps teach newcomers archery and gives them a feel for the sport during ODFW's monthly archery Outdoor Skills classes. "We really encourage people that have some interest in archery but never tried it to come out," said Swartz. "We can teach them how to hold the bow and aim and shoot. So we get a lot of youngsters and women too, folks who've never shot a bow, try it and seem to like it."

It's the sort of experience that may put your youngsters right on target for new adventures in the Oregon outdoors and by all accounts, thousands of folks have renewed interest in this ancient sport that puts each individual in control of their actions. At Tigard's Archers Afield—one of Oregon's largest indoor shooting ranges—twenty-eight lanes are jammed with youngsters learning how it's done. Manager Kris Demeter said that young imaginations are fueled by movies like *Brave* and *The Hunger Games* whose main characters discover independence and self-reliance with a bow and arrows. "We have many teenage girls coming in that want to resemble or be like the main characters they see in those two movies. They want to wear the back quivers or shoot the longbows—it's remarkable," noted the longtime manager.

Demeter is an accomplished archer who has been the archery instructor at Archers Afield for the past 27 years. Newcomer Gabe Bolden said that he learned something new his first visit: "I learned that instead of standing flat square facing the target, it's best to turn for a better aim—it's true."

Back at John Strunk's Tillamook workshop, he agreed that the learning never stops, and that's a good thing. It keeps the sport fresh, engaging, and exciting. He remains motivated to build more bows and shoot more arrows. "It becomes a passion and that's what it's all about for it helps to build lifelong friendships too—I've many brothers in archery. Who couldn't have fun doing this?"

You can reach out to Strunk's Spirit Longbows (503-842-4944) to learn more about building bows and arrows. He teaches classes in the craft throughout the year. Traditional archery is more popular than ever and you can find clubs and shooting ranges across Oregon to give it a try. If you are interested in learning how to shoot modern bows, try the Oregon Bow Hunters association.

28A E. E. Wilson Wildlife Area

Where: 29555 Camp Adair Road, Monmouth, OR 97361
Web: dfw.state.or.us
Phone: 541-745-5334

28B Archers Afield

Where: 11945 SW Pacific Highway, Suite 121, Tigard, OR 97223
Web: archersafield.com
Phone: 503-639-3553
Watch the Episode: traveloregon.com/archery

A Fall Expedition

K ids love the old-fashioned Sunday drive! They really do. It's their chance to get out of the house and bond with family members, so set the electronic gadgets aside, turn off the radio, and get ready to teach your kids about the fun that can be had along back roads without numbers—some of the very best around.

An October sunrise across the Jewell Wildlife Area is cool and crisp and quiet . . . but not for long! Elk bugling is unlike any trumpet that you've ever heard, according to Wildlife Area Manager Bryan Swearingen: "All bull elk will bugle but the majority of the bugling that you hear out here during the rut is from the mature bulls because they are dominant and actually run the smaller bulls off. The bulls bugle at one another, they challenge one another, then they kind of pace side by side."

Swearingen added that there are many other signs that the rut, or elk breeding season, has arrived. "The bull elk will square off and then all of a sudden they turn and lock their antlers with each other and push against one another. It goes on, back and forth for several minutes, and the elk really mean business until one of them finally gives up."

It isn't a fight to the death, but a pushing match that determines strength and virility in the herd. The bull elk grow antlers up to 5 feet high with a tip-to-tip spread that's even wider. As hormones rise, the bulls become more aggressive and alder tree rubs are common: "I think the tree rubs color up the antlers and it also lets the elk burn up some of their aggression. It also helps establish herd dominance," said Swearingen. "If they tear up a tree, it says to the other elk I'm meaner than you so stay away from me."

Jewell Meadow is also home to deer, coyote, hawks, songbirds, and even bald eagles, which may be visible in autumn to the patient and keen observer.

Don't stay away from Oregon State Highway 202—a roadway where leaf colors change each day! Stephanie Beall, a recreation specialist with the Oregon Department of Forestry, noted that the timing couldn't be better: "It is gorgeous out there right now! The vine maples are brilliant oranges and reds while the alders and bigleaf maples are turning amazing shades of yellow . . . you're going to see some amazing color."

It *is* amazing and there's more just off US Highway 26, at milepost 35, where you can pull into a spacious parking area sporting a new information board with a trail map to guide your family to one of the most unique Oregon hiking destinations called Four County Point Trail (managed by the Oregon Department of Forestry, Forest Grove District, 503-357-2191).

The mile-long hike is manageable for even young children, especially when the goal is to reach a granite monument that marks the only spot in Oregon where four counties meet. Beall offered, "The trail parallels a creek for a bit, so sometimes if you're out in the early morning, you may see deer or other wildlife."

Once you reach the monument, you can straddle the site and admire Clatsop, Tillamook, Washington, and Columbia Counties—all in a heartbeat—a fun cap to an easy hike and a geographic feature you won't find anywhere else in the state.

You can also dive off Highway 26 at Elsie, Oregon, and head down a narrow lane past limb-framed farms that cry photo op before it zips past softly rounded hillsides on which trees sport what calendars told us nearly a month ago: the seasons are changing! The Nehalem River's tributaries also show you the changing times: some start as tiny, spring-fed trickles across spongy moss that later grow giant and creek-sized and where husky salmon have muscled their way back from the salty sea to find their birth home in time to spawn.

"It is so exciting, you just don't want to leave, can't stop watching them," said local photographer Don Best, who was perched above popular Nehalem Falls at the Oregon Department of Forestry's Nehalem Falls Campground (Foss Road milepost 7, Nehalem, OR 97131; 503-368-3803). (*Note*: the campground closes for the fall-winter season, but the trail to the falls remains open.)

Best is an avid fan of the site and tries to capture the salmon show each fall. The water handsprings over unseen rocks through the falls while other river spots show off a distinct river's rhythm that provides a source of restoration for the life that grows here. "I'll be here for hours trying to get that 'oooh-ahhh' shot," said the longtime outdoor photographer. "They jump high and they jump low and you never know where they'll show up. Plus, they're only in the air for half a second so you don't always get them in the perfect shot. Some people take pictures underwater and they turn out really great—but to get them flying through the air is a different story—that's fun for me." That's the nature of back road byways where uncertainties wait at every turn and what you might find makes the best adventure.

28C Jewell Meadows Wildlife Area

Where: 79878 Highway 202, Seaside, OR 97138
Web: dfw.state.or.us
Phone: 503-755-2264
Watch the Episode: traveloregon.com/FallCoast

November

29

The Oregon Connection

Oregon has a banana belt, a near tropical landscape along the state's south coast, but you won't find pineapples or mangoes or papayas growing there. Instead, you'll find plenty of cedar, fir, and even giant redwoods—plus, one particular hardwood variety that grows from south of Reedsport through Northern California and east from the Coast Range Mountains to the I-5 corridor: myrtlewood!

My connection with Oregon myrtlewood is by way of family. My grandmother Dee Sturdivan collected many beautiful and useful myrtlewood pieces, mostly for kitchen table use: salt and pepper shakers, a lazy Susan for varied tableware, and even a few select pieces that were far more "fancy" than anything else she owned, including a small clock, a few serving plates, and even a myrtlewood cribbage board. Her collection was well tended and cared for and I always admired the gleam of the wood but never quite understood her love for so much myrtle. The fact was few of our other relations had as many myrtlewood pieces in their homes, so I think my grandmother took pride in that. For me, the presence of myrtlewood in my grandmother's home has provided a lasting page from the book of childhood memory.

Bowls like this connect me to childhood memories of my grandmother's myrtlewood collection.

I recall asking her one time about her collection and for her, it was simply an

The Myrtlewood Grove Trail is an easy hike at Alfred Loeb State Park.

"Oregon connection" that she could not resist. She never really explained what it connected her to, but I suspect she was drawn to the simple beauty that the finished wood pieces offered. I also think she collected myrtlewood pieces from her rare travels across Southern Oregon and along the southern Oregon coast, mementos of distinct getaway vacations for a woman of simple tastes that also provided her a lasting memory of something purely Oregon.

Your family can find easy-to-reach stands of myrtle along the southern Oregon coast. The first is a hike through a myrtlewood grove at Alfred Loeb State Park. It's an easy trail that winds through 40 acres and offers visitors a chance to see and smell the largest public-owned old-growth myrtle stand in the state. "It smells like camphor or eucalyptus," said Park Ranger Jean Phillips. "In fact, if you crush the leaves, it'll clear out your sinuses real fast—it has that kind of strength! It's a distinctive and a clean smell that's unique to our campground." There is also a nice trail along the Chetco River and plentiful picnic tables. The campground is open year-round and has forty-seven electrical sites, three reservable cabins, and restrooms and hot showers. One of the cabins and one campsite are ADA accessible.

The second stand is 24 miles east of Coos Bay on Coos County Road 241 where you become a part of the Glenn Creek watershed in a towering old-growth myrtlewood forest. It is so significant a place it has been deemed "protected" as the Millicoma Myrtlewood Corridor since 1949. You pass through the corridor to reach a somewhat hidden and lesser-known state park property called Silver and Golden Falls State Natural Area. "It is at the end of a long road that is fairly narrow and winding but it is passable," said Park Manager Preson Phillips. "It's an unassuming parking lot with a restroom and some trail signs. The trails to each of the falls are relatively flat and easy hiking for one-third of a mile each until you hear the roar! Those are the falls."

At 254 feet, Golden Falls is among the tallest waterfalls west of the Willamette River—its spray and sound leave you breathless. At 130 feet, nearby Silver Falls is a joy to watch, and together they have been called the two most impressive waterfalls in Oregon's Coast Range. When you see them after a heavy rain, it's difficult to argue. Golden Falls fiercely roars into a box canyon and gushes out sprays that offer multiple rainbows when the afternoon sunlight hits just right. Silver Falls, in contrast, spills out over an ancient basalt porch and seems to stream in mesmerizing rivulets.

Myrtlewood is a distinctly Oregon wood and its shavings really fly when craftsman Rey Martinez carves a block of it. Martinez has been carving myrtlewood for more than 20 years. He uses steel tools called gouges, scrapers, and chisels on his lathe to turn myrtle blocks into fine bowls, plates, and even tables! "It's a dying art, the turning of myrtle on a lathe—and not many guys do it anymore," noted the longtime craftsman from his workstation at the House of Myrtlewood in Coos Bay, Oregon. "I started 'turning' myrtle about 6 months into the job but it took me awhile to really perfect my style," added Martinez. "I love creating many of the popular items because the wood is so beautiful. I like bringing out the beauty of the wood."

Finding the beauty in the wood has been every carver's goal ever since House of Myrtlewood opened in Coos Bay in 1929. Back then, they sawed myrtle logs into giant slabs and then into wood blocks that carvers transformed into gift shop goodies for tourists to take home. "Myrtle is a very hard wood," noted store manager Stacy Gavette. "So it is great for cutting boards and other utility uses. It is also beautiful because each piece is a different color. Myrtle can be blonde or dark brown and there's no staining of it. We don't want to cover the look of the myrtle because it's so fantastic on its own." The House of Myrtlewood is open Monday through Saturday in the winter (Sundays too, in the summer) and allows visitors to take a self-guided tour that begins with a 12-minute video (with free popcorn) showing all the processes in the factory from rough log to finishing. Following the video, you can tour the drying room that features historic photographs as well as myrtlewood pieces from years past. You can also tour the rough woodworking area and main shop with turning, sanding, and branding of the wood. The best days for the tour are Mondays through Thursdays when the shop is in full production.

Martinez is one of a handful left in Oregon who carves myrtle full-time. He said that the wood is really "wet" when it arrives in the shop because myrtle retains moisture. So it must be dried out for nearly 3 months before he can carve an inch.

In the workshop, under loud leather belts and clanking steel wheels that have run the lathes since the Great Depression, Martinez will turn out dozens of bowls in a day. He hands each bowl to coworker Mychal Berry, who finishes the pieces with ever-finer sandpaper and then applies a coat of mineral oil to bring the myrtle to life. Some pieces are marked by fiddleback contortions in the grain that look like undulating waves and give the bowl a washboard effect. The finished myrtlewood bowl is gorgeous and it's easy to see why people fall in love with them. After all, each provides the new owner a little piece of Oregon created by local craftsmen who take tremendous pride in their work.

29A Alfred A. Loeb State Park

Where: N Bank Chetco River Road, Brookings, OR 97415
Web: oregonstateparks.org
Phone: 541-469-2021; 800-551-6949

29B Silver and Golden Falls State Natural Area

Where: Glenn Creek Road, Coos Bay, OR 97420
Web: oregonstateparks.org
Phone: 541-888-3778; 800-551-6949

29C The Oregon Connection—The House of Myrtlewood

Where: 1125 S. 1st Street, Coos Bay, OR 97420
Web: oregonconnection.com
Phone: 541-267-7804; 800-255-5318

Watch the Episode: traveloregon.com/OregonMyrtlewood

30

Just for the Kids

Families who like to ramble, explore, and generally hang out in Oregon's forests may wish to visit two sites that bring out the adventurer in each of us—but you should know: this getaway is for kids . . . of any age at a forested parkland where your views can feel a bit like a bird's-eye view to the woods. It's a perspective that will take your breath away: up to 60 feet off the ground! It is found only at the unique Tree to Tree Aerial Adventure Park set in the foothills of the Oregon Coast Range in western Washington County.

The Nature Play Area is a natural for youngsters who like to play outdoors.

The 57-acre forested parkland is unlike anything you've ever experienced off the ground. In fact, you might consider it a playground *in the trees*. Instructor Patrick Murphy guides folks across the four different tree-to-tree courses—each course is progressively more challenging and he helps people find steady steps on a shaky trail or across a swinging, swaying wobbly way. Murphy said, "This is something that kids like to do—they like to come out and be active, climb in the trees—use their imaginations—pretend to be monkeys or Tarzan or whatever . . . all sorts of fun stuff built for young and old to play up in the trees." Each climber

Tree to Tree Adventure Park offers swaying bridges, tunnels, and rock walls that you can climb.

must wear a safety harness that connects with two lanyards sporting lobster claw–type clips that in turn link you to thick wire cables. Each cable can hold up to 10,000 pounds, so once you're clipped in—you're not going anywhere except across the aerial trail.

The Tree to Tree Park is a family-owned business, according to co-owner Molly Beres. She said the park's location (a short drive from Scoggins Valley Park and Henry Hagg Lake) has attracted a following once visitors discovered their park's unique features. "Portland is the best place for this sort of thing because there are so many outdoorsy people here. Everyone likes to be outside doing active things and extreme sports and this will fit in just fine." The park also offers a course for climbers as young as 7 with the same elements as the adult version but it is much closer to the ground. The course admission is based on age and height; that is, if you are at least 10 years old and able to reach 5 feet (with your arms extended overhead) you can play on the full-sized course after you've passed the Basic Training Course.

Youngsters able to reach 5 feet and ages 7 to 9 can play on the smaller course. There is also an Adventure Village tree fort playground and mini obstacle course and Monkey Grove climbing gym in the trees for children ages 2 to 7 (a child must weigh at least 35 pounds for Monkey Grove). The park's many course features are called elements and range from simple swaying bridges to horizontal rock walls and tunnels that you must climb across or climb through to continue the course.

Many participants agreed that the climbing experience felt safe despite the 50-foot elevation and that it is an experience full of surprises: First-timer Pete Conklin noted, "It definitely tests your balance and your fear of heights—makes you a little nervous—but all of it is doable."

That feeling never lets up on the course either—it's surpassed only by the thrilling payoff that waits for each climber at the end. "We end every course with a zip line and so it's the payoff for your hard work because everybody loves a zip," noted a smiling Beres. "Our whole purpose is to be outdoors, enjoy nature, and enjoy being in Oregon—just to love where you are—it's the best!" A full zip line tour is available (weight limit between 75 and 250 pounds; no height restriction) as well as the aerial obstacle courses. They even have racing zips where you can race your friends and a challenge called the Plunge for anyone over 50 pounds who wants to experience a 15-foot free fall before being slowly lowered to the ground. The zip lining safety tips outlined in chapter 2 apply here too. Some people prefer to wear gloves while going through the courses, but they are not sold at the park, so plan on bringing your own from home.

In true Oregon fashion, the park is open rain or shine, but will close during high winds or lightning. Lockers are available during summer months. Reservations are required as are parent waivers for children under 18 and one adult is required to remain on the premises. If you're not feeling the call to climb the courses, you can walk the trails at ground level (stick to the trails to avoid poison oak) or rest at one of many chairs or picnic tables. You can even pack in your own lunch or buy snacks at their welcome center.

Another great option with the kids is Silver Falls State Park's Nature Play Area, and when you visit you may wonder: how is it I've not been here before? "One of the things we see happening is kids coming over here and building forts," said Oregon State Parks Manager Steve Janiszewski. "That's OK! We want to see that. We want their parents to come out here and play with their kids too." The park has installed the natural play area designed with play "pods" mimicking the habitats of native animals.

At each pod, marked with a colorful jumbo-sized totem pole, kids can experience what it's like to be a bear clambering into a log den, a bird shaping a nest out of twigs, or a cougar tracking a deer through the forest. Stuart Rue and Sarah Evans brought their two young boys, Archer and Anders, to explore the play area and they had a blast! The purpose of the play area is to get kids outside and engaged with nature, as well as to spur creativity and promote a better understanding of animal capabilities and interactions between species.

"It's got a nice blend of the traditional play elements with the nature elements and I like that," said Evans. "We try to do a lot with our kids outdoors and we love to go camping, hiking. We all love being outside." Silver Falls State Park's Nature Play Area is the first of its kind in an Oregon state park and more are planned in the future. The park also has many year-round family-friendly activities including 25 miles of hiking, mountain biking, and horse trails; waterfalls and a creek; picnic facilities and barbecue stands; horseshoe pits; an off-leash area for dogs; and reservable camping sites for tents, RVs, and in cabins and dormitory-style bunkhouses.

30A Tree to Tree Aerial Adventure Park

Where: 2975 SW Nelson Road, Gaston, OR 97119
Web: tree2treeadventurepark.com
Phone: 503-357-0109
Watch the Episode: traveloregon.com/treetotree

30B Silver Falls State Park

Where: 20024 Silver Falls Highway SE, Sublimity, OR 97385
(The Nature Play Area is at the north end of the park.)
Web: oregonstateparks.org
Phone: 503-873-8681; 800-551-6949
Watch the Episode: traveloregon.com/JustKids

31

Islands in the Sky

I was 8 or 9 when I caught my first views to the two stunning landscape features called Upper and Lower Table Rocks. I was on a family camping trip and we were on our way to meet relations in the Medford area before heading into the nearby mountains. I recall great curiosity about the two mountains that looked like their tops had been chopped off and wondered aloud why my dad called the landmarks "Islands in the Sky." I wondered how it might be possible to touch the sky,

Boardwalks allow visitors access to wetland areas atop Lower Table Rock.

who might live way up there, and how I might get to the top of the two prominent sites. I also recall asking my folks about visiting the sites and the unified response that followed: "No way, too much poison oak along those trails."

It would be many years before my professional career offered an opportunity to visit the two sites. In the late '80s I met with representatives from The Nature Conservancy on a news story that explored the unique botanical qualities of the sites and explained why The Nature Conservancy purchased more than 4,000 acres of Table Rocks and why they deemed the properties worth protecting as preserves.

A note of caution is due here: my folks were absolutely right about the amount of poison oak that grows up the sides of the Upper and Lower Table Rocks: it is everywhere alongside the trails, so when you take your kids to explore the sites, be sure they stay on the trails. Even a short straying off-trail risks an itchy rash that affects most folks who encounter poison oak. Staying on the trail also helps you avoid ticks and the occasional rattlesnake while protecting the area's vegetation.

More recently, on a day too nice to stay indoors, the trail to outdoor learning was opened wide when I joined The Nature Conservancy's Molly Morrison and the Bureau of Land Management's Molly Allen for a tour to the top of Lower Table Rock; the two women were prepping volunteers who would soon be leading grade school students on tours of the site.

It was a wonderful hike and I could not help wondering why this visit had taken me so long to repeat. In spring months you can count on a broad variety of wildflowers on showy display: shooting stars, fawn lilies, and red bells were always by our sides. But at any time of year, there's also plenty of elbow room for brushing up on botany and wildlife, like the wild turkeys that may strut across the fields adjacent to the trail.

Up to 5,000 students visit here each spring, summer, and fall and hike the nearly 2-mile-long trail to the top of Lower Table Rock. As we began our hike, Allen noted, "From down here on the trail, you can see the gently sloping sides. This is where the softer sediment is eroding from Lower Table Rock. It's a really unique landform that's so different from anything else around Southern Oregon."

Seven million years ago, a nearby volcano erupted and filled the ancient Rogue River Valley with lava. Over the millennia, ancient rivers eroded the landscape but left these two plateaus (not mountains) behind. Each Table Rock (Upper and Lower) rises more than 800 feet from the valley floor. Each Table Rock is also protected by the co-owners, the Bureau of Land Management (BLM), and The Nature Conservancy as Areas of Critical Environmental Concern. "That designation means that it can't be developed," added Allen. "There cannot be resource extraction like logging or mining here because of the special plants and animals that live here."

Once you reach the top of Lower Table Rock, it is easy to see that the plateau is wrapped by ancient basalt and offers eye-popping views of the valley floor below. Peering down to the ground on the plateau, you can see a main trail that leads to scores of vernal pools that fill with rain. "These pools are like fascinating aquariums," said Morrison. "They are full of small invertebrates including the star of the show, fairy shrimp or vernal fairy shrimp, that are cute little critters." The Table Rock fairy shrimp are classified as a threatened species because of loss of habitat.

More than 200 wildflower species grow on Lower Table Rock including the extremely rare dwarf woolly meadowfoam. "That flower only grows on the top of the Table Rocks and nowhere else in the whole wide world," added Morrison. The Lower and Upper Table Rocks are indeed like "islands in the sky"; they are iconic features for the region, landmarks of natural and cultural history that are dearly loved by residents and visitors alike.

Trails to the top are open year-round and the Table Rocks Education Program brings student groups frequently during school hours. In addition, free guided hikes are offered to visitors in April and May. Three- to five-mile round-trip guided hikes along a moderate grade trail generally last 3 to 5 hours. Anyone is welcome to sign up, but reservations are required. Space is limited to twenty individuals. Contact the Medford District BLM (phone number below) to reserve a spot. There is no drinking water at the trailhead and no restrooms at the top, so be prepared. Also be aware that in order to protect this resource and prevent erosion, Table Rocks are off-limits to pets, bicycles, and motorized vehicles. And be sure to use designated cleaning stations to remove seeds, plant parts, and mud from your boots and clothing both before and after your hike; this helps prevent the transfer of invasive plants and animals.

Travel Oregon is involved in educating visitors at the Lower and Upper Table Rocks too. The organization's Forever Fund recently provided a grant to The Nature Conservancy to replace aged information kiosks. The new signs will provide both natural and cultural history as well as geologic facts about the two unique features that are truly Oregon wonders.

31 Table Rocks

Where: Just north of Medford, OR off SR 234
Web: blm.gov/or/resources/recreation/tablerock
Phone: 541-618-2200 (Medford District BLM)
Watch the Episode: traveloregon.com/SkyIslands

32

Child's Play for All—Oregon Dunes National Recreation Area

When my sons were young, I made a point of finding Oregon destinations for our visits and I would often set my family's travel compass for the southern Oregon coast near Florence, where we discovered a perfect family-based campground at Honeyman State Park. Honeyman boasts history dating back to the 1930s, when the Civilian Conservation Corps built the massive stone and timber lodge along Cleawox Lake. Swimming and fishing continue to dominate the recreation scene at this Sahara by the sea. Nearly 300 campsites for tent or trailer await you at Oregon's second-most popular state park.

According to retired State Park Ranger Mike Rivers, there is a certain allure to this park beyond all the other coastal campgrounds: "We like to call Honeyman a destination vacation, and I think that's because people generally enjoy it since it's so centrally located to many other adventures. They come to play in the sand, of course, but many come to boat and fish [there are scores of freshwater lakes and streams close at hand] and use our picnic grounds. Many campers are third generation—and that's neat. But, of course, the big reason they all come is the sand dunes."

Towering sand dunes, some reaching 400 feet in height, are among the highest in the world, and miles of flat beaches stretch as far as the eye can see. Together these two features distinguish the Oregon Dunes National Recreation Area (ODNRA). Camping, hiking, horseback riding, fishing, birding, and designated areas for off-road vehicles can be enjoyed in this 42-mile stretch from Florence to Coos Bay, where the ocean coast meets the mountain forest.

Marty Giles is my go-to person when I really want to learn about the southern Oregon coastline in general and the Oregon Dunes in particular. She owns

At 14,000 acres, the Oregon Dunes extend more than 2 miles inland and some dunes reach 200 feet tall.

and operates Wavecrest Discoveries (wavecrestdiscoveries.com, 541-267-4027) in Coos Bay and can really set you straight about natural history, marine biology, botany, and geology. Plus, she knows the best place to catch a crab, dig a clam, or cast a line. I've known Marty for many years, and many times she's saved this forlorn reporter with some important tidbit of information about her vast backyard sandbox called the Oregon Dunes. Not long ago she told me, "It's like no other place in the world because it stretches along the coast in a narrow band. Sand certainly makes it all happen, but lush forests also grow on it, and water runs through it, and ponds and lakes are dammed up and formed by it."

Marty met my family and me one late September afternoon at William M. Tugman State Park, 10 miles south of Florence, for an eco-hike into the dunes. Ecotouring is Marty's specialty, and she explained that to really understand how all 32,000 acres of sand happened in the first place, you have to hike into the dunes to see the wind and the water in action.

"Millions of years ago most of Oregon was under water and had a sandy sea floor. Over time this sea floor was pushed up and became the Coast Range [about 12 million years ago]. The heavy rain and winds of the Pacific Northwest eroded the sandstone, then rivers carried it to the ocean, where the sand now extends at least 150 feet offshore." As we stood gazing to the ocean from a high dune Marty estimated to be about 200 feet tall, she continued. "As the waves and high tides carry the sand onto shore, it's dried by the sun and blown back inland. The present shoreline stabilized 6,000 years ago, but the tides, wave action, and strong coastal winds moved sand up to 3 miles inland over the thousands of years since." Marty added, "Nature came together in some pretty amazing ways to create this unique phenomenon. That's not to say there aren't problems—and one of the biggest is European beach grass!"

You can see the problem of beach grass just about everywhere throughout the dunes. It was first planted to prevent sand from blocking rivers, streams, and roads. But today it's spread all along the coast and has become a barrier to sand movement from the beach.

"For many that's a good thing," added Marty. "But for the natural order of life that's evolved over thousands of years to a sandy habitat, it's a huge disruption. Some animal species, like the endangered snowy plover (which builds its nest in the open sand), lose out when the sand disappears. Biologists say the grass is moving an average of 22 feet per year across the sand, and plants may entirely cover the dunes during the next 150 years. It's a tough management problem."

Oregon Dunes National Recreation Area encompasses 14,000 acres of sand dunes containing scores of lakes, streams, parks, and campgrounds, extending along the Pacific Ocean from the Siuslaw River south to the Coos River. At its widest point, the dunes extend inland approximately two and a half miles.

One convenient location for getting oriented is the Oregon Dunes Day Use Area and Overlook, 11 miles south of Florence. It's one of the few sites within the recreation area where motorists can stop and see the dunes without making an extensive side trip. The overlook is situated between US 101 and the beach and was designed barrier-free so that it is fully wheelchair accessible including a paved trail to picnic areas. Visitors can view the Oregon Dunes and Pacific Ocean from a series of observation platforms or you can venture across the dunes themselves. Restrooms are available at the overlook. Visitors can also learn about many of the recreation activities and features of this vast sandy playground with a stop at the ODNRA Visitor Center in Reedsport, at the junction of US 101 and Oregon 38.

Just off US 101, Tugman State Park is something of a hidden gem along the marvelous south coast. Situated on Eel Lake near the community of Lakeside, Tugman offers ninety-four campsites with electric and water hookups tucked away in a mature stand of shore pines. The day-use area has a restroom and gazebo-style shelter surrounded by broad green lawns with plenty of space for large and small groups. The waters of Eel Lake are outstanding for fishing, swimming, canoeing, sailing, and boating. A trail around the south end of the lake allows hikers to get away from the developed area of the park and to explore the lake's many inlets. Maybe you'll catch glimpses of osprey, heron, eagle, deer, or other woodland creatures as you walk through forests of spruce, cedar, fir, and alder.

Eel Lake offers many fishing opportunities. The brush-lined shore and steep drop-offs make it the perfect lake for a bass boat and bass fishing. The lake has a good population of largemouth bass (some weighing up to 5 pounds) and other fish. A fully accessible fishing dock can be accessed from the day-use area near the boat ramp. Trout and bass are often caught from the dock. Tugman State Park is a great place to camp with kids because sixteen yurts are available (eight of which are pet friendly; reserve in advance) and there are hot showers, restrooms, a picnic area, and a playground.

32A Jessie M. Honeyman Memorial State Park

Where: 84505 US Highway 101, Florence, OR 97439
Web: oregonstateparks.org
Phone: 541-997-3851; 541-997-3641 (campground booth); 800-551-6949

32B Oregon Dunes National Recreation Area Visitor Center

Where: 855 Highway Avenue, Reedsport, OR 97467
Web: fs.usda.gov
Phone: 541-271-6000

32C William M. Tugman State Park

Where: 72549 US Highway 101, Lakeside, OR 97449
Web: oregonstateparks.org
Phone: 541-759-3604; 800-551-6949

Watch the Episode: traveloregon.com/SouthCoast

December

33

Hooking Kids
on Steelhead

Oregon's late fall and winter seasons are often marked by cold winds and driving rain—even sleet or snow can be the main entrees on the state's winter weather menu. Still, there's a certain breed of Oregonian who say, "There's no better time to be outdoors!" Jack Glass says the Sandy River makes you wonder how a river 30 minutes from downtown Portland lets you feel a million miles away from city hubbub? Part of the answer may be found in the day's fishing crew: Kennedy Shuler, Grant Embre, and Tess Raz.

Although young, their enthusiasm and interest in fishing was easy to spot—all eyes were on Glass's every move as they listened intently to each word of instruction that he offered on how to cast. "You want to slowly bring the rod back behind you," said the longtime fishing guide. "Then—pause for a moment—and cast. You don't need to cast far—maybe 20 yards toward the bank. Let it hit the water and close the spinning reel's bail."

On this recent gray-shrouded December morning, marked by intermittent showers and a temperature hovering near 40 degrees, Glass shepherded the boatload of youngsters up and down the Sandy River. An accomplished pro fishing guide (hookupguideservice.com, 503-260-2315) with more than 4 decades of experience on Oregon rivers, he said he never tires of taking youngsters fishing for steelhead. He especially loves to watch a youngster catch their very first!

His strategy: encourage kids at every turn with gear they can handle—a simple bobber and bait and a technique called bobber doggin'. "It's a pretty forgiving way to fish," said Glass. "Throw the bobber out there and when it disappears you swing—jerk as hard as you can. So it's a pretty easy deal for the young ones to handle." Glass is a big believer that if you give a kid a rod and reel—show them how it works, you'll get them hooked after the very first bite. Twelve-year-old Grant Embre didn't have long to wait—his bobber sunk after his first cast: "Fish on, fish on! Grant has a fish on," yelled our guide. A streaking silver flash erupted from the river as a 10-pound steelhead put on quite an acrobatic show. Soon, the gleaming steelhead was in the net and Glass exclaimed: "See what I mean! Kids listen, they really listen—you tell them to do something and they do it. It's terrific fun to take kids out on the river because they absorb the information and follow instructions."

"It's not just fun for us kids," said the beaming Grant. "It's also fun for the parents. Even if you don't catch fish, it's fun to be on the river because you might see wildlife like bald eagles—you also get a break from the TV and video games."

We were soon underway again and rounded a bend in the river. Glass slowed the boat and said, "Ah, this spot here is what we call 'Powerline Drift.' A real sweet steelhead spot—kind of shallow with a little bit of an island, but an all gravel bottom—perfect spot to intercept a steelhead."

Steelhead are oceangoing rainbow trout that can reach 20 pounds or more! Anglers prize them for strength, stamina, and endurance—there's simply no finer fish on hook and line. Many devotees call them the street fighters of the anadromous (migrating from saltwater to spawn in freshwater) fish world because they often travel the farthest and endure the harshest environmental conditions in order to reach their spawning areas that are located high in the watershed.

"We use a spinning rod and reel, cast close to shore, and then drift along the bank in the boat, said Glass. "We really use the boat to present our baits. The more water you cover the more chances you have of presenting it to more fish, so this method of moving downstream presents your gear to more and more fish. That adds up to more catching!

"There you go, jerk, jerk, jerk!" shouted Glass. "Kennedy has one—go, girl, go!" The fish rushed up and down the stretch of river that Glass had chosen for us. Kennedy held the rod tip high as the reel's drag applied just the right amount of pressure and the 15-pound test line held tight. She soon had the fish under control and near the boat. Glass slipped the net under the fish and brought it aboard. It was a dandy 8-pound *hatchery* steelhead. How could Glass tell the fish was born in a hatchery? "All of the hatchery fish have their adipose fins [a smallish, half moon–shaped fin located between the dorsal fin and the tail] clipped before they're released from the hatchery as babies," he explained. "So look back by the tail and you can see this fish doesn't have one—so it's a hatchery male steelhead and it's absolutely gorgeous."

I asked Kennedy to describe the feeling of hooking and playing a steelhead.

Youngsters sport mile-wide smiles when they hook and land winter steelhead.

"It's a good feeling—it's like a challenge to get it in the boat. I really like that challenge because it isn't like anything else." The three kids' dads were out on the river too. They watched the action from a distance. As we continued our fishing trip, Glass told me that the Sandy River offers good bank access for anglers too. That's especially true at parklands like Dabney State Recreation Area and Oxbow Regional Park—and even farther upriver. Dabney Recreation Area also has a disc golf course that is open year-round and it has picnic and beach areas that are popular in summer months. Oxbow Park is also an enjoyable year-round destination with 12 miles of hiking trails, several covered reservable picnic areas with barbecues, fifty-seven drive-up and ten RV camping sites (two of which are accessible), heated restrooms, hot showers, and a playground. Note that pets are *not* permitted in either park.

Glass insisted that boaters should practice good sportsmanship and allow bank fishermen plenty of elbow room. The Sandy River is born high in the glaciers of Mt. Hood and it is a river that keeps boaters on their toes because river safety is critical. "Quite often there are trees that come down because of windstorms or freezing weather conditions," explained Glass. "They can even block entire channels, so you've got to be aware all of the time whether you drift or jet boat the river." He added that folks who choose to ride with him play it safe by wearing inflatable life jackets throughout their trip. The life jackets are so lightweight, you hardly know you're even wearing one.

Within moments of Glass's comments, 11-year-old Tess Raz's bobber disappeared under the surface and her fishing rod doubled over and throbbed with the pulsing fight of an 8-pound, nickel-plated steelhead. "Ohhhh, nice fish . . . man oh man, it's gorgeous!" Glass yelled, as monofilament screamed off her reel. "She's got a real barn burner on her hands." Glass smiled, I laughed, and Tess seemed a bit nervous. She did not want to lose this fish. Tess had tied into a dandy and she handled the rod like a pro.

Her dad, Art Raz, said he had made outdoor time a priority with his daughter from an early age: as soon as she could walk she joined him for fishing adventures. His advice to other parents: "Make the time and spend the time with them! You have to because they grow up way too fast. Every time I hooked a fish I handed her the rod and now—as you can see—she's catching more fish than me."

Tess soon had the fish to the boat and Glass scooped it aboard—it was a fine hatchery steelhead. I asked her what she enjoyed the most about steelhead fishing. "Well, you can have really good family experiences and sometimes—like today—you'll make a lot of fun memories."

That's a fine piece of impressive wisdom from a youngster who truly understood the values that come from fishing—it's not always about the catch, but about the time you spend outdoors learning and experiencing something new. Glass smiled and added, "These young folks are the future for our sport—and especially managing our resources—engaging them in activities like fishing makes a huge difference down the road and for the future of angling in Oregon."

33 Dabney State Recreation Area

Where: Historic Columbia River Highway, Corbett, OR 97019
Web: oregonstateparks.org
Phone: 503-695-2261; 800-551-6949

Oxbow Regional Park

Where: 3010 SE Oxbow Parkway, Gresham, OR 97080
Web: oregonmetro.gov
Phone: 503-663-4708; 800-551-6949

Watch the Episode: traveloregon.com/SteelheadKids

34

Forest Grove Santa

When I was young, I fell in love with teaching. I had many terrific teachers who influenced my decision to follow the educator's path—both high school teachers and college professors who prodded and challenged me to learn, especially history, biology, and literature. My favorite teachers led me to discover the rewards that come from learning, and in turn, shaped my plans to share my knowledge as a teacher. In fact, I taught in public school for 5 years and I continue to teach at the college level.

When I made the move to broadcasting in 1982, I told my friends and family members that my teaching career was not over, but that my classroom simply grew larger. It's true! Through the years, the opportunities to teach folks about Oregon have allowed me tremendous freedom to travel and learn and share my stories. I have paddled, soared, hiked, biked, climbed, flown, dived, swum, crawled, and—yes—driven tens of thousands of miles in trucks, jeeps, and vans, on motorcycles, and inside buses and RVs across a region reaching east to the Rockies and north to Alaska. For the most part, my story assignments put me face-to-face with interesting characters, intriguing destinations, and a menagerie of wildlife from eagles to whales, salmon to elk, and even to cave-dwelling bats. Most of us rarely see such a wide array of critters and can only imagine

Each Christmas, Mickey Johnson plays a timeless and generous role that also supports a great cause.

In December, Mickey Johnson's front yard becomes the North Pole and he becomes the Forest Grove Santa.

such wild adventures. Mine has been a dream job, akin to a year-round Adventures 101, where class is always in session and the homework chronicles spectacular places and amazing activities.

Forty years ago, in the earliest days of my teaching career, I was mentored by a real pro, Mickey Johnson, who was my supervising teacher during a semester of student teaching at Forest Grove High School. Johnson was a longtime language arts teacher who covered writing, speech, drama, and much more. He was a big believer in making connections in kids' lives—not just teaching the academics, but presenting young people with options through extracurricular activities. Indeed, he was the high school drama teacher for 35 years and he directed hundreds of plays, designed and built the sets, and helped thousands of students *discover* school from a different point of view—on a stage!

But Johnson's passion for the stage took him in another direction too. Each December, he dons the red suit and black boots and grows out a snow-white bushy beard that brings mile-wide beaming smiles to hundreds of kids. He plays a role that is timeless, generous, and supports a great cause. His visitors range in age from 1 to 92 as they line up in his front yard that's transformed into a Santa set for five nights just before Christmas. Johnson's "work" begins in July when woodworking tools come out and his imagination travels to a "North Pole" that he builds in front of his home. He is the Forest Grove Santa, spreading good cheer and exuding the holiday spirit. "I built the first sleigh nearly 20 years ago," he recently explained. "Each year, I've added a few more pieces. I buy lights on half-price sale and then spend the next year trying to figure out what I'm going to do with them. Eventually, it fills up the whole yard."

This is no ordinary season's greeting from a kindhearted man, but something more important. You see, in 2001, Johnson's daughter, Barbara, was diagnosed with leukemia, but went into remission after taking a regimen of drugs developed at the Oregon Health and Sciences University. Johnson wanted to give back and his idea seemed right at home for a retired drama teacher. He built a sleigh, found a costume, and became a Santa. Now, he warms the cold winter air with his good cheer as he greets all who stop by his Forest Grove yard. "I wear long johns and fleece pants under the suit—if it's really cold, I'll put a couple of toe warmers in my boots."

Rain, snow, hail—even windstorms—he's been through the worst the outdoors can dish out for nearly 2 decades and yet, he's never missed a December performance. "People bring their kids and sit them down on Santa's lap and take pictures. We have a big sock here and folks can leave donations for the Oregon Leukemia and Lymphoma Society. This is my little contribution—whatever we can do helps a little bit. This is a good way of paying back for what the doctors gave us. It's that important to me, so someone else's child might survive too."

His Santa rendition has raised thousands of dollars for cancer research but he insisted that all his efforts pale in comparison to what a youngster with cancer endures. He gets to entertain kids with a merry ho-ho-ho and spark their imaginations as Jolly Saint Nick. He said he's now playing Santa for the children of people he used to play Santa for when they were younger. "Some kids can hardly wait, you can see them coming down the street running," Johnson said. "One year, I had a girl whose parents couldn't convince her to get in the sleigh and see me. She came back the second night and came up to me and took a candy cane. She came up the third night and sat in my lap. By the fourth night, I think she was all over me and didn't want to get out of the sleigh."

It is a payback to the delight of kids of all ages and a personal thank-you that lives year-round in the soul of a good-hearted man called the Forest Grove Santa.

34 Forest Grove Santa

Where: 1901 Willamina Avenue, Forest Grove, OR 97116

35

Forgotten Ghost Towns
and New Beginnings

Back roads are the best when they lead you down trails to Oregon's secret hideaways that provide rich history lessons that continue to teach today. Tracking down Oregon history blends well with travel across the state. It's the travel that lets you roam into townsites, villages, or communities that barely exist . . . some that history buff Steve Arndt calls ghost towns that are rich with history about the shaping of the state.

For example, when the Sumpter "Stump Dodger" steam train engine blows its whistle, one thing is certain—you'd best be on time or you'll miss the ride! "Last call! Train Number One to Sumpter departing in 5 minutes!" said Sumpter Railroad conductor Daniel Bentz. The young man strolled across the wooden planks of the McEwen Depot and played his part well in a period costume and a full-on character performance. He continued, "So hurry and buy a ticket—then step aboard the Stump Dodger because even a century later, this railroad is always on time."

Up to three times a day, Baker County's Sumpter Valley Railroad makes the 12-mile round-trip run from McEwen Depot to Sumpter, Oregon. The railway runs Memorial Day through October, plus special trains in December and other holidays; special events include train robberies and photo specials. The round-trip takes about 2 hours. Riders of all ages are welcome and children under 5 don't need a purchased ticket. It's a railroad that reaches back to the early days of settlement in Northeast Oregon, according to the railroad's operations manager, Taylor Rush: "The railway meandered in and out of every canyon throughout the Sumpter Valley as it followed the timberline in the 1880s. In those days they said the railroad engine would dodge the stumps as it crawled up into the mountains and that name just stuck."

For the price of a ticket you can ride across a unique chapter of Oregon's past: a gold mining past marked by a giant dredge that chewed up the North Powder River Valley and pulled 9 tons of gold out of the ground. Square-bowed and built of steel and wood and iron, three giant dredges lifted and sifted the terrain, reaping a golden harvest worth $12 million during the peak of the Depression era. Today, the dredge stands as a silent sentinel of the past and takes visitors aboard to see and touch gold rush history at the Sumpter Valley Dredge State Heritage Area.

"Each bucket [there are seventy-two total] on this dredge would pick up about 9 cubic feet of material. It would wash the gold off the rocks and would drop through into some sluice boxes and then out the back," said Park Ranger Garret Nelson. Inside the heart of the dredge—big as a barn and filled with gears and belts, winches and pumps—the rock passed through steel cylinders, separating rocks by size before water and sluices separated the gold from the dirt. Nine tons of gold in 20 years!

Oregon's back road byways are the best! Across north Central Oregon, less than 20 miles south of The Dalles, you quickly see that distances are great and the people are few and times gone by are easy to find. I found a good ghost town where the sun shines 300 days a year. It's only 90 minutes from Portland yet feels a million miles away from city clamor and noise. Oregon history buff Bob Waldron said that the Friend School—built in 1909—offers a sneak peek to the promising life that folks wanted to find when they settled in this part of the Oregon country. "Life here could be dirty, bad, nasty, and too short," said Waldron. "But it held the promise of a new beginning. The availability of land was—for a lot of folks—the opportunity to start a new life."

At Friend, Oregon, in Wasco County, "life" reaches back to the 1870s. Named for a local homesteader, Friend was the sort of place that flourished for a moment and then disappeared: "One of the beauties of Eastern and Central Oregon is that there are still lots of places like this—where you can find plenty of elbow room and live in solitude," added Waldron. "It's not for everybody, obviously, or everybody would be out here, right? But—look around. It is gorgeous."

He's right! Wasco County offers stunning country. White River Falls State Park has a sprawling greenway with scattered picnic tables at a day-use site that opens each spring and closes in the fall, but you can venture here in the winter by parking on OR SR 216 (don't block the gate) and hiking to the viewpoint. Be sure to use extra caution with the kids as the icy trail can be very slippery this time of year.

Friend, Oregon, flourished for a moment then disappeared, but the
Friend Schoolhouse stills stands as a community center.

You'll be drawn to explore the rugged quarter-mile trail that takes you riverside where you discover something more: A complicated system of pipes and flumes diverted water from above the falls down into a powerhouse and where electricity-producing turbines generated power for the region from 1910 to 1960. The Dalles Dam construction and completion led to the White River project's demise and it shut down in the '60s.

For obvious safety reasons, Oregon State Parks does not want visitors inside the old powerhouse building that is falling in upon itself. "Keep Out" signs on the shuttered building make that message clear, so observe the signs as you explore the riverside scenery. Do not forget a camera or cell phone when you hike this path for the photo ops are numerous and stunning—of the river, the canyon, and the powerful White River Falls where two plunge-pool falls drop more than 90 feet in dramatic fashion at this time of year. The park is a popular picnicking, hiking, and fishing retreat for visitors who wish to dip their toes in this corner of the greater Deschutes River corridor.

Historian Steve Arndt insisted that even more valuable riches are waiting for families to find anytime across Oregon. "Well, first of all," explained the retired college teacher, "Oregon has more ghost towns than any other state . . . 256

of them—some are well-known like Sumpter—but many more towns are really obscure, like Friend." By his own admission, Arndt has been a ghost town buff since he was a youth and tagged along with his dad who would scour the countryside for old townsites. The bug really bit Arndt at an early age. "For me, a true ghost town has buildings but no people, and one of the buildings needs to be a church, a school, a store, or the post office."

Arndt has made finding and learning about Oregon's past easier than ever in a series of books: *Oregon Ghost Towns: A to Z* (roadslesstraveledoregon.com). The books include real time-tested treasures too! Like Golden, Oregon. A true ghost town that's but a stone's throw from the popular Wolf Creek Inn, an Oregon State Heritage Site located near Grants Pass, just off I-5. While the inn is temporarily closed, the grounds are open for exploration and picnicking. There is a portable restroom, but no water service. "Golden, Oregon, was never really a town—more like a mining camp," noted Arndt. Golden was a booming place in the 1850s when millions of dollars in gold was dug or power-washed out of nearby Coyote Creek. At one time there were as many as twenty-five buildings including several homes, a general store, a blacksmith shop, a school, and a church. Remarkably, four buildings remain standing at the Golden State Heritage Site today. "The Golden Church is especially worth your time to visit," added Arndt.

Arndt advised that you don't have to travel far to find an Oregon ghost town for many sites are easy to reach on short drives from Portland into the Willamette Valley—like McCoy, Oregon. Arndt led us into a concrete building that seemed more a bunker than a former working rail line building: "This is one of the old booster stations from the electric railway days and these booster stations were located about every 5 miles up and down the rail line." Oregon's Electric Railway was ahead of its time in the early twentieth century. The electric railway connected Portland with Eugene and many smaller towns throughout the greater valley. Towns like McCoy flourished for a time because they were so well connected with the outside world and it was easy to ship goods and products. The Oregon Electric Railway era ended in the late 1940s. Arndt explained, "The diesel trains were quick, carried more freight, and all these little stations along the line gave up the ghost and became ghost towns."

He's right! There are scores of old Oregon townsites to find, explore, and admire—some, like Hopewell, Oregon, are marked with a storefront or two that have somehow managed to endure the decades. Arndt's ghost town adventures provide plenty of places and information to ponder and wonder. Plus, as you explore more of Oregon, you have the chance to know the place you call home.

"It's funny," said Arndt. "Not only do I look at the buildings and the structures that have lasted, but I often think about the tears, the laughter, and the people who had lives in these buildings. As people have souls, I think community does too."

Arndt is adamant that holding on to Oregon's past is important—not only do we get to know this place we call home, but without understanding where we have come from—we risk losing ourselves in the future. It's important to remember that these places are important links with Oregon heritage, so it's best to take nothing but pictures and memories and leave nothing behind but footprints when you visit.

35A Sumpter Valley Dredge State Heritage Area/ Sumpter Valley Railway

Where: 211 Austin Street, Sumpter, OR 97877

Web: oregonstateparks.org; sumptervalleyrailroad.org

Phone: 541-894-2486; 800-551-6949; 541-894-2268 (Railway)

Watch the Episode: traveloregon.com/sumptervalley

35B White River Falls State Park

Where: Maupin, OR 97037; 45.241666,-121.094444

Web: oregonstateparks.org

Phone: 800-551-6949

35C Wolf Creek Inn State Heritage Site

Where: Old State Highway 99S at Front Street, Wolf Creek, OR 97479

Web: oregonstateparks.org

Phone: 800-551-6949

35D Golden State Heritage Site

Where: Coyote Creek Road, Wolf Creek, OR 97497

Web: oregonstateparks.org

Phone: 800-551-6949

Watch the Episode: traveloregon.com/wolfcreek

36

Marine Life Center

When my sons were young, I was always more successful at teaching through some hands-on demonstration of what I could not explain with words. So imagine my great pleasure on a recent visit to the University of Oregon's new Marine Life Center in Charleston, Oregon. It's an absolute wonderland of marine science for kids and parents and grandparents, a visit that's made for the curious. "Visitors of all ages are so interested and so excited to be here, but they may not know enough about the Pacific Ocean off the Oregon coastline, especially the organisms that live there," said Carly Salant, a marine biology student who works as a teacher and guide at the new center. "So my favorite part is being able to teach them and that gets them excited. They even spread the word and even more people come."

They are coming by scores each day to not only see but do hands-on learning with marine samples that can be viewed under microscopes or you can lend a hand during feeding time or use the interactive exhibit that allows you to match the right whale with its correct call in the ocean. Salant added that the 2-million-dollar museum and aquarium is the only one of its kind on the southern Oregon coast where visitors are greeted by full-size skeletons. "And these are the real things— right up front is a toothed whale orca and right behind her is a juvenile gray whale. They make for a pretty impressive entrance to the center."

"The center is about the diversity of ocean life," Trish Mace, the center's director, said in a statement. "We want to introduce people of all ages to the incredible diversity of life in the waters off Oregon, and also to the research being done by faculty and students at the University of Oregon and the Oregon Institute of

Marine Biology." The UO's marine biology presence on the coast dates to 1924 when the Oregon Institute of Marine Biology was established and it has operated on a 100-acre site in Charleston since 1931. The new Marine Life Center (MLC) offers interactive lessons on coastal ecosystems, deep-water habitats, and diverse sea life through hands-on, shallow touch tanks with starfish, anemones, and sea urchins. As Salant and I stared into one of the aquaria, she observed, "We have a large cabezon right here and we've also got a purple sea urchin here on the window that you can see. The rocky reef represents the type of habitat you'd find right off the Oregon coast, the reef area right offshore."

If you time your visit during the lunch hour, you'll have a chance to watch student Rachel Prescott feed an array of marine life: from young octopus, varied rockfish, an amazing basket sea star, and a rarely seen Puget Sound crab. "Feeding time is great" said Prescott. "It creates a feeding frenzy for the guests that come too; you get to see how the animals eat, exactly what they eat. The techniques they use are so unique and really incredible—it's the most popular time for kids and adults. I love my job. There's never a dull moment, that's for sure."

The center includes five separate galleries spread across two stories. Between them, they focus on coastal ecosystems, deep-water habitats, marine mammals,

Youngsters can satisfy their curiosity about marine life at the Marine Life Center's tide pool touch tanks where visitors are encouraged to poke around.

fisheries, and diverse sea life with genuine artifacts and ocean habitat supplied by the institute's teaching labs. There's an open-air covered fisheries gallery that allows visitors to see the comings and goings of fishing vessels while interpretive panels show the process that various local fisheries undergo. The two-story 6,400-square-foot building was built entirely from donations and it is a place that will teach you much about our coastal waters. It should not be missed. "It's the great collection of people that work here and those folks who come through to visit," added Salant. "I hope more people will make time to visit us soon."

"It was important to me to explain the story of the Charleston fisheries and the fact that we're in an area with a big presence of Native Americans and that we're on or close to their ancestral lands," said MLC Director Trish Mace. "You feel like you're part of the harbor . . . like you're on a ship. Charleston and Coos Bay have outstanding access to marine habitats. It's just a perfectly situated place to study marine biology and a remarkable opportunity for students and it's a beautiful small museum." The center is open Wednesday through Saturday from 11:00 A.M. to 5:00 P.M.; children are admitted for free.

---

36 Charleston Marine Life Center

Where: 63466 Boat Basin Road, Charleston, Oregon 97420

Web: charlestonmarinelifecenter.com

Phone: 541-888-2581

Watch the Episode: traveloregon.com/CharlestonMarineLife

Winter

Grant McOmie's Outdoor Talk— Caring for Oregon's Wildlife

Throughout my travels as an outdoor reporter the past 3 decades, few people have impressed me more with their passion and sense of purpose in caring for the critters than the kindhearted woman who found her life's calling in the rural countryside near Astoria in Clatsop County. I first journeyed to the Wildlife Center of the North Coast to meet Sharnelle Fee for a special television program in December 1998 (following many positive reports I'd heard about her successful wildlife care efforts) only to arrive in the midst of a surprising and terrible storm. A powerful cold front aimed straight at Oregon had raced out of the Gulf of Alaska. It was staging a relentless attack on the coastline with 90 mile-per-hour winds building massive, endless breakers that rolled and exploded onto shore. This was a time when nature was at its spectacular roughest, and yet it was against that backdrop of coastal wildness that I found a remarkable back eddy of calm at her small wildlife hospital.

Fee was a big believer that abundant and varied wildlife are a measure of a community's environmental health. She owned and operated the facility that is located on more than 100 acres of forested land along the Youngs River near Astoria. She described the center's mission simply: "Each year, we have wildlife species that get into trouble and our jobs are to make them well." There was no paid staff in those early days of operation—all of her assistants were volunteers and the remarkable 2,500-square-foot wildlife hospital with a 350,000-dollar price tag was paid for by grants and donations. Fee credited the local community and the many people who believe wildlife at risk deserve all the help we can give them: "It takes will and determination to care for wildlife."

That was the nature of Fee's commitment to help wildlife, birds large or small—from murres to cormorants to pelicans—that showed up on her doorstep. Fee told me that her mission was "to help the sick or injured critters recover from whatever ails them." I also learned that "raptors and rifles" constitute a common theme at the care center too. In fact, scores of wounded birds are brought to the clinic each year, and Fee is able to patch up many of them for release back to the wild. But for a not-so-lucky few, fate has determined another path. The otherwise healthy birds become ambassadors of sorts for wildlife education programs. As we walked and talked, Fee proudly described her many resident birds, including a mature bald eagle whose right wing was but a mere stub of its former self—another gunshot wound, this one causing an amputation. "The raptors get into trouble by flying into power lines or they are hit by vehicles or sometimes people just shoot them for fun too," said Fee. For nearly 20 years, the center has been an oasis of aid for these birds, led by a modest woman who believed the best in people can be measured by their commitment to help the wildlife that live in the outdoors. Sadly, Sharnelle Fee passed away on September 14, 2015, after several weeks of battling a severe lung infection.

I recently met with the new Wildlife Center director—Josh Saranpaa—(he served as Fee's assistant for many years, starting when he was in high school) who said that the work of the 12-person volunteer staff will continue to handle thousands of birds each year. In addition, volunteers conduct about eighty educational programs every year, teaching the public about seabirds and raptors. Volunteer Donna Wren described her reason for helping: "The love of animals. That's the biggie right there! This was all new to me when I started 2 years ago, and I learned—I still learn something new about wildlife every day."

Volunteer Melissa Corvin said that they will go through hundreds of pounds of small fish called capelin each week: "We feed our birds exactly what they would find in the ocean." Saranpaa added that too often no amount of fresh fish helps. You see, increasingly, seabirds like northern fulmars show up near starvation because their stomachs are filled with small bits of plastic! "Something like 85 percent of the fulmars we took in last year had plastic inside them. The sharp pieces perforated their internal organs and the plastic leaches toxins and make them sick. When they are full of plastic they can't eat to fill up their stomachs properly."

Yet—their work makes a difference: I have personally witnessed the release of small seabirds called murres, pelicans, and even a bald eagle that discovered freedom in flight again—brief but rewarding moments that bring the center's caregivers back each day. I will always remember Fee's expression of commitment summed up in a response to my simple question: "What motivates you?" She paused—gave the question serious thought and replied: "People are such a difficult species to live with. I want to be more than a consumer . . . I want to give back to this earth and make up for things that I consumed . . . and make a difference on the planet."

January

37

Base Camp Baker

Tommy and Diamond will give you a ride through Baker City that you won't soon forget—the two giant Percheron horses are well-muscled and known for "their intelligence and willingness to work," according to Ron Colton, who at nearly 80 years young, held tight on the reins to the giant horses. "I really like the Percheron draft horse," he noted. "They are a little bit more docile than all the other breeds."

Colton is a man that locals call the "real deal" in Baker City; he's a cowboy and horse wrangler who has worked with draft horses most of his life. These days—he and his sidekick, Barbara Sidway, are teachers who share the town's history on weekly horse-drawn tours—rain, shine, or snow! "We thought this idea was a great one because it is too much to walk through the town," said Sidway. "And driving doesn't allow the time to see enough—it's too fast! So a horse-drawn tour of our town is just right."

Sidway is owner and operator of Baker City's landmark Geiser Grand Hotel. It was built in 1889 and its elegance will spoil you. There are fine crystal chandeliers, rich mahogany millwork, and a spectacular stained glass atrium. Plus, thirty guest rooms that invite you to linger longer. Your family will feel right at home here as the welcoming staff will gladly share with your kids any of the couple dozen old-school board games they have on hand, or lead you to the reading library complete with a shelf of kid-friendly titles. They have a collection of a thousand family-friendly DVDs that can be checked out and viewed in your room—you can even order up room-service popcorn and soda or an epic ice cream sundae. If mom and dad want a night on the town, the hotel has a credentialed child care provider on

Percheron horses Tommy and Diamond give visitors a fun and memorable history lesson about Baker City.

call to provide babysitting services in your room. And you can even bring the family dog; they are a pet-friendly hotel with complimentary food and water dishes, treats, and a dog walk.

Behind the hotel is a 3½-mile walkway along the Powder River that connects two parks—one provides steps down to the river and the other features large shade trees and a playground. Hotel staff will even help you plan one of many exciting side trips during your stay. Called Real Adventures, these trips include an amazing array of activities from the horse-drawn carriage tour to experiencing life on a ranch to feeding buffalo to mountain biking and hiking to ghost hunting.

Back out on the town's streets, as the hooves meet the pavement, Sidway seemed right at home aboard the large wooden wagon. She said that she loves sharing Baker City's remarkable story. "Baker City is the largest intact nineteenth-century streetscape in the American West. There are more than 100 buildings on the National Registry of Historic Places, so this tour is like visiting a museum of Victorian architecture. The horses provide the perfect pace to get to know it."

Sidway said Baker City escaped the boom and bust cycles that plagued many Oregon towns over the past century. Plus, the current population of nearly 10,000 people hasn't changed much in the past 120 years. Most of all, the town was so wealthy from gold and silver mining, the city built landmark stone structures that endured. One such building offers a welcome stop and the chance to meet Davey and Alyssa Peterson, who have a love affair with rich, delicious chocolate.

The two locals have traveled the world but they came back home 5 years ago to open a business that blends their passions for art and sweet chocolate (Peterson's Gallery and Chocolatier, petersonsgallery.net, 541-523-1022). In the kitchen, we were treated to a sneak peek of Alyssa's daily truffle-making process. One of her prized recipes combined cocoa powder, cinnamon, and chili powder that covered a rich ganache that's 65 percent pure dark chocolate. "I am always experimenting with something new and it is fun to surprise customers who will sample a truffle and suddenly a unique flavor pops out," said the longtime chocolate maker. Alyssa said she learned her way around the kitchen at an early age from parents who loved to travel and eat.

Her chocolate truffles are out-of-this-world delicious. In fact, they were so good, I offered to move in and go to work for the couple—for free! Everyone laughed at my offer—and yet I remain hopeful and my offer stands! "For me," added Alyssa, "chocolate making is like creating a masterpiece painting every day. I can make the same piece each day and lots of people will enjoy it."

Back on the trail, Sidway added that Baker City sits at a crossroad for Oregon adventures. In fact, many call the historic town Base Camp Baker for the many activities waiting at every turn. "Consider us your base camp to explore our region! There are so many more things to do than you can find the time for." One must-see stop is the National Historic Oregon Trail Interpretive Center located just 5 miles east of Baker City. During winter months the center is open Thursday through Sunday and is loaded with hands-on exhibits that tell the story of the Oregon Trail. Rotating exhibits allow your family to "experience" the trail with activities like trying on pioneer clothes or packing a replica wagon or discovering the wildlife you might have seen along the trail. Nearly every day a brief program illustrates what life was like for the pioneers (the program varies each day). Additional special events occur throughout the year. Youth age 15 and younger are admitted free.

Also open on weekends during winter months is the Baker Heritage Museum (2480 Grove Street, Baker City 97814; 541-523-9308; bakerheritage-museum.com) with exhibits that help visitors learn about the history of the people and the Baker City region including Chinese culture, mining, timber, ranching, agriculture, and wildlife. And you may want to stop by the Chinese Cemetery and Memorial on Windmill Road (just east of I-84, exit 304). Interpretive signs at this site explain some of the story of Chinese immigrants in Baker County.

37A Geiser Grand Hotel

Where: 1996 Main Street, Baker City, OR 97814

Web: geisergrand.com

Phone: 541-523-1889; 888-434-7374

Watch the Episode: traveloregon.com/DowntownBaker

37B National Historic Oregon Trail Interpretive Center

Where: 22267 Oregon Highway 86 (Exit 302), Baker City, OR 97814

Web: blm.gov

Phone: 541-523-1843

38

A Jewel Anytime—
Diamond Lake and Crater Lake

Oh, Dad—I wanna go, I wanna go. Pulleeeeeaassse, can I, can I, can I?"

My then 10-year-old's sorrowful eyes coupled with a mile-wide grin were working their magic on me.

"OK, OK," I relented, "but you have to sit right here and hold on to me real tight! I mean tight!"

Bundled in snowsuits, boots, and helmets, Kevin and I were quite a blimpy looking pair as we assumed our positions in the line-up of purring snowmobiles. More than a dozen folks, patiently waiting aboard their idling snowmachines, were ready and anxious to begin the 2-hour guided tour around Diamond Lake.

Diamond Lake in the southern Oregon Cascades is a jewel of a destination that I've enjoyed visiting since I was a young boy, although most of my childhood memories of the lake have centered on camping and fishing and balmy summer nights. Not so long ago, I invited the family for a December adventure at Diamond Lake to discover that the multifaceted playground attracts nearly as many folks in the winter months.

Rick Rockholt, former manager at Diamond Lake Resort, had advised me to schedule our travel midweek, when there were fewer visitors. He met us with a hearty handshake and an eagerness to show us around on a day of clear blue skies and glistening snowfields. He shared that the tradition of service and family fun began in 1922, when Diamond Lake Resort was strictly a fishing lodge, but the resort has developed into a year-round destination.

"When Diamond Lake freezes over and then is blanketed with snowy powder, this place becomes a winter wonderland. There are so many different ways to enjoy the snow, too, from skiing to snowshoeing to dogsledding.

Snowmobiling at Diamond Lake is one of my favorite Oregon winter activities.

You'll never hear the kids say, 'I'm bored up here,' for there's way too much to do for that nonsense."

We discovered he was right. Seven miles of groomed trails and thirty-five miles of backcountry trails make this a wonderland for cross-country skiing and snowshoeing (rental equipment is available), but other opportunities also await. Once unpacked and situated in our cozy room at the resort, we were quickly out the door and headed for the number-one family activity at Diamond Lake's Hilltop Tubing Center. Each of us was awarded a supersized inner tube and a tow clip for unlimited rides down a wickedly thrilling tube run about a quarter mile in length. The three boys plopped one after the other—first with body facing forward, then backward, then sideways, half on, half off—for ride after ride after ride down the snowfield. The tubing hill is open during the week for 5 dollars, but be aware that the uphill tow doesn't run so you have to walk back up. The tow operates Friday through Sunday: $15 for 2 hours; $20 for 3 hours; $25 for 4 hours; $30 all day. Recent upgrades include a 470-foot wonder carpet conveyor lift and seven lanes with new faster tubes.

I could have stayed there all day, but an earlier commitment to join Rockholt for the snowmobile tour meant leaving the family on the slope. When word slipped out that a snowmobile could carry two, the boys vied for that special second position. After a short ceremony of the "me, me, mes," the youngest brother, Kevin, won out, but I noted how quickly the other two rebounded: With a loud shout of

"Kowabunga!" each plopped onto his tube and with a roar of laughter blasted out of sight for the umpteenth time.

Snowmobiles are a great way to get around Diamond Lake's snow country, and the area has become a favored destination for the Northwest's snowmobile crowd. Between the resort and the Oregon State Snowmobiling Association (oregonsnow.org), more than 300 miles of trails are groomed each week. The sport has also enjoyed tremendous growth in the past decade as the machines have become easier to operate and ride, even for the first-time rider. All the trails are open to the public and most visitors bring their own sleds, but Diamond Lake Resort offers a variety of guided tours and do-it-yourself rentals.

One of the most popular tours departs Diamond Lake four times each day to zoom out and around Diamond Lake and then continues 20 more miles on the northern approach to nearby Crater Lake. The National Park Service permits snowmobile use at Crater Lake National Park only on the North Entrance Road from the park boundary to North Junction, where the entrance road meets Rim Drive. At Rim Drive we stopped and stepped a few yards across the snow to take in one of the most magical winter sights I have ever witnessed—Crater Lake in winter! The spectacular view—the lake's brilliant blue, defined by an apron of snow folding from the rim down the steep canyon walls to a very distant shore—was overwhelming for its size and sublime beauty.

It also stirred my imagination about all the power and fury of the incredible events that occurred here 7,000 years ago. That was when Mt. Mazama erupted with lava and magma shooting toward the sky. The mountain collapsed, leaving the bowl-shaped caldera in its place. Over the ages, the bowl filled with snowmelt and rain and became the wonderful lake we love and admire today. We gazed across the lake for a much-too-short 20 minutes before Rockholt nudged us along for our return. Kevin was in heaven for the thrill of a snowmobile ride with Dad, surpassed only by the stunning size of majestic Crater Lake.

---

38 Diamond Lake Resort

Where: 350 Resort Drive, Diamond Lake, OR 97731 (check website for directions as this address is generally not recognized by GPS).

Web: diamondlake.net

Phone: 541-793-3333

Watch the Episode: traveloregon.com/diamondlake

39

Cape Foulweather—
Where Oregon Began

T he Pacific Coast Scenic Byway is a roadway of discovery that reaches into playgrounds for hiking, camping, and wildlife watching, plus miles of sandy shoreline and rugged rocky headlands at a place "where Oregon began!" That's especially true along the central Oregon coast at a place whose name strikes to the very heart of the winter season: Cape Foulweather!

"Foulweather is probably one of the most popular and picturesque areas along the Oregon coast," noted Oregon Parks and Recreation Department Ranger Dave Newton. "Everyone who visits wants to get that prime photograph and right here they can do that." Rising 500 feet above the ocean, Cape Foulweather—"where Oregon began"—is the first Oregon land formation that Captain Cook spied in

The view from atop Cape Foulweather offers offshore rocks and tide pools.

The "Fairweather Coffee Bar" was built in 1937 and later became a gift store that's now operated by the Oregon State Parks Department.

March 1778. Cook coined the name for the fierce weather and rough ocean conditions that he and his crew encountered. Cape Foulweather is an Oregon state park that offers a fine perch with fabulous views to bald eagles and gray whales.

Newton added that the Cape Foulweather gift store's history reaches back nearly a century when Buck and Ann Badley built the place as a coffee shop: "They named it 'Fairweather Coffee Shop,' but they found out that wasn't really what the people wanted. Folks wanted souvenirs that they could take back with them, so the Badleys changed it into a gift store." Oregon State Parks acquired the site in 2013 and quickly made changes: "We wanted to open up the store's space and give visitors more opportunity to enjoy the views," explained Newton. "So we cleared shelves away from the windows and put in benches and binoculars that invite people to stay longer. And they do!" The gift store is a great place to take a break and warm up with the kids while still being able to enjoy a panoramic view.

Nearby, you'll find many good reasons for an even longer stay. Beverly Beach State Park Campground offers 280 sites for tents or trailers—plus twenty-one yurts (ten of which are pet friendly) that offer many of the same comforts of home. Three of the campsites and six yurts are also ADA accessible. The park has restrooms and hot showers and a visitor center where you can purchase firewood. There are hiking trails, picnic areas, and a playground. Plus, there's easy access to the sand that gives families miles of beach to stretch out and play.

A short 4-mile drive to the south leads you to the sprawling Yaquina Headland. A site that is managed by the Bureau of Land Management (BLM) as Yaquina Head

Outstanding Natural Area, each spring it is home to seabirds by the thousands—plus, the site offers some of the most accessible tide pools of the Oregon coast.

"The tide pools at Yaquina Head are probably the most diverse," said BLM Ranger Jay Moeller. "They have probably the most living things in them of any tide pool that I've seen in the Northwest. Really diverse and easy to get to and they're protected." Above it all, Yaquina Lighthouse has stood its ground since 1873, and today visitors line up to go inside on guided tours. BLM Ranger Bret Greenheck said he gets a kick out of playing the part of a Yaquina Lighthouse keeper and guiding folks up to the top. "The winds across Yaquina Headland can typically reach 100 miles an hour," said Greenheck. Our walls in here may whistle but they do not waver!" You'll not waver on your visit to this stretch of scenic byway. The sun and the surf and the sand make certain it's a place that's never twice the same.

Five short trails on the headland give your family opportunities to watch for whales, take in panoramic views, scour a cobblestone beach (please leave the stones on the beach), or make your way to the Quarry Cove observation deck to watch harbor seals. The Yaquina Head Interpretive Center offers exhibits discussing the history of the area and also houses a gift shop and restrooms. Park rangers give scheduled tours of the lighthouse and tide pools. Call the park for dates and times.

39A Otter Crest State Scenic Viewpoint/ Lookout Observatory and Gift Shop

Where: Otter Crest Loop, Depoe Bay, OR 97341
Web: oregonstateparks.org
Phone: 541-765-2270; 800-551-6949

39B Beverly Beach State Park

Where: US Highway 101, Newport, OR 97365
Web: oregonstateparks.org
Phone: 541-265-9278; 800-551-6949

39C Yaquina Head Outstanding Natural Area

Where: 750 NW Lighthouse Drive, Newport, OR 97365
Web: blm.gov
Phone: 541-574-3100

Watch the Episode: traveloregon.com/CapeFoulWeather

40

Memories Matter

In 2017, it's hard to believe that there was a time not so long ago when wooden, concrete, or steel bridges were uncommon features across Oregon rivers. In fact, only short-span covered wooden bridges were a part of the Oregon landscape in the late 1800s as more than 500 ferries carried people, wagons, and agriculture across the state's many rivers. "Almost every pioneer community, especially in the Willamette Valley, was connected to their neighbors by roads crossing at least one river on a ferry. Ferries were a fact of Oregon life in the nineteenth and early twentieth centuries. For many people, the memories of that travel matter," said Bob Waldron, board member of the Oregon Maritime Museum.

Today, only a handful of active ferries remain in service and perhaps that's why I've such a love affair with these remnants of an earlier, simpler bygone era. Moreover, I remember traveling each of these ferries as a youngster and it felt like high adventure as I recall begging my parents to take me back to the other side of the Willamette River—"let's do it again and again," I'd plead on the short river crossing at Wheatland Ferry, near Salem. I think youngsters feel a sense of power and energy from the rumbling ferry engine—an absolute thrill best enjoyed by families seeking outdoor adventure in their travels.

THE DANIEL MATHENY ON A GAS TANK GETAWAY

My television reports entitled *Gas Tank Getaways* have long been a favorite of mine for their convenience and lasting enjoyment. The unique out-'n'-back adventures won't break the bank on auto fuel, and they are the kind of exciting activity in which the journey can afford as much pleasure as the destination. I'm especially

The Tourist No. 2 *has traveled across the Northwest in her near century of service but now she has returned to Astoria*

fond of the trips that breeze along some of Oregon's finer back roads across the landscape of Willamette Valley farmlands.

Perhaps you'll get as much of a kick out of this picture as me when you travel high on the spine of a ridgeline to find two spectacular views for the price of one stop at Bald Peak State Scenic Viewpoint (Bald Peak Road at Holly Hill Road, Hillsboro, OR; oregonstateparks.org; 503-678-1251). At nearly 1,700 feet in elevation, Bald Peak offers a miles-wide checkerboard perspective on Willamette Valley farmlands to the east. On a clear day, you can pick out three Cascade peaks, including Mt. St. Helens, Mt. Hood, and Mt. Jefferson. If you step a hundred yards to the west and glance over to the Tualatin Valley, you'll also see the rising Coast Range just beyond. In a soaring grove of Douglas fir, take your pick from dozens of picnic tables scattered here and there. To the east of a vast parking area, stroll across the open grass meadow that serves as the peak's namesake. This marks the perfect site for an afternoon picnic lunch, though no drinking water or flush toilets are available in this park. From atop Bald Peak, a wavy ribbon of asphalt carries your four-wheeled land schooner south 15 miles to Dayton.

From Dayton, stay on Oregon 221 for approximately 8 miles and pull into Maud Williamson State Recreation Site (SE Dayton-Salem Highway, Salem, OR 97304; oregonstateparks.org; 503-393-1172), where enormous Douglas firs shelter the picnic sites and a rough-hewn post-and-beam timber shelter can be reserved

The Daniel Matheny *river ferry will carry on average 600 cars
and trucks across the Willamette River each day.*

for larger groups. This is a park that's entertained families since 1934, when the Williamson family donated the land to Oregon. (*Note:* That's the family's white-washed home that still dominates the scene.) Maud Williamson is a wonderfully shaded recreational oasis. The park is equipped with toilet facilities, volleyball and horseshoes are available, plus there's lots of room to roam. The ease of access from Oregon Highway 221 makes it another ideal site for a quick lunch stop.

The park is pleasant, but there's more for the curious just around the bend and a quick dash down an intersecting lane to the Wheatland Ferry dock. This is where the *Daniel Matheny* river ferry drops her steel gate, unloads her passengers, and quickly takes on more for the short ride across the broad Willamette River. The flat-bottomed *Daniel Matheny* is based at a once-functioning pioneer wheat port, but it is far from a nostalgic tourist attraction. It's all about the business of transporting vehicles and commerce: an average of 600 cars and trucks a day, and during peak periods commuters and farm trucks may wait as long as 20 minutes to make the 5-minute crossing. A ferry has operated here since 1844 and pedestrians cross for free, while vehicles—including bicycles, pay a toll. So it really is possible to park your car and ride back and forth for free, much to the delight of your children.

Once you've landed on the Willamette's western shore, it's only a matter of a mile to reach the entrance to rambling Willamette Mission State Park (Wheatland Road NE, Salem, OR 97304; oregonstateparks.org; 503-393-1172): 1,680 acres of fantastic picnic opportunities and many group sites for larger crowds, making it a long-favored destination for family reunions. You'll find a wide variety of natural settings and accommodations for varied recreation at this day-use park including a bike path, hiking trails, horse trail, disc golf, boat ramp/fishing, wildlife viewing, and ADA-accessible restrooms (no individual overnight camping allowed, but open from dawn to dusk daily; small entrance fee charged during the peak of tourist season—Memorial Day to Labor Day—larger fee to reserve group picnic shelters). Plus, nearby Mission Lake is ideally suited for gentle canoeing (no motors allowed). Eight miles of trails wind throughout the park with an incredible number of native birds, plants, and wildlife.

This parkland also offers many photo opportunities, including one of the oldest trees in the state. A massive cottonwood tree stands 158 feet high with a canopy that spreads more than 110 feet wide. The circumference at the trunk is more than 27 feet, and the limbs are as big as most tree trunks. The gnarly bark resembles plowed furrows that stretch hundreds of feet into the air. Some estimate the tree dates back to 1735. Taking a moment to stand beside it and feel its age is a worthy pause.

You may wish to consider the role this historic area played in Oregon's early political and religious development too. Willamette Mission is named for the site where in 1834 pioneer Jason Lee established the Oregon Territory's first Methodist Church. Although nothing remains of the original buildings, follow the well-marked trail to an interpretive plaque that explains Lee's role in early Oregon. It's a peaceful place with a fine wooden bench on which to sit while taking special note of a rambling pink rose bush that grows near the plaque; it descends from the original bush that was planted near here almost 170 years ago.

Where Wanders the *Oscar B*

Many years ago, I asked then-Captain Olaf Thomason if he ever grew weary of the twenty daily trips back and forth across the broad-shouldered Columbia River onboard his 60-foot charge, a ferry then called *Wahkiakum*. "Why not at all, Grant!" With a knowing wink, the gray-bearded skipper smiled and added, "This is better than any ride you'll ever find at Disneyland."

The *Wahkiakum* ferry was retired in 2015 and replaced with the *Oscar B*. The ferry operates 365 days a year, a minimum of eighteen runs per day. The *Oscar B* arrives on the quarter hour at Westport, Oregon's steep-walled shore, to let loose her small troop of travelers before she takes on more. On one splendid winter day, when barely a riffle was felt across the smooth, slippery surface of the "Mighty Columbia," I rolled my family rig across a thick steel accordion-like crossing plate and onto the ferry.

After a half-dozen fellow travelers and their cars were secured aboard, the gate rose with a boom and we began our 20-minute crossing. It was pleasing to see the willows and alders and cottonwoods that line the banks of the Columbia. The river had lulled all of us into thinking life was pretty grand on a day so pleasant. "Payback!" I told the family, "for all those gray-shaded, drizzle-choked winter days when it's nearly impossible to ever see the riverbanks, let alone distinguish one side of the Columbia from the other."

Puget Island was our landing point, and then we drove a short way into nearby Cathlamet, Washington, which serves as *the* gateway to a wildlife destination you may have missed on Washington State Highway 4. The Julia Butler Hansen National Wildlife Refuge consists of nearly 6,000 acres of diked Columbia River floodplain and un-diked islands, backwater sloughs, wetlands and ponds, splendid spruce forests, and open grass meadows. The refuge is a wintering area for tundra swans, Canada geese, and several species of ducks. Watch for resident bald eagles, migratory warblers, and other songbirds. Other waterbirds and raptors are common, so be sure to bring your binoculars, and the surrounding waters hold salmon, steelhead, sturgeon, and trout.

All of this is fine, but my number-one reason for making the refuge a family getaway is to see and learn more about a little-known endangered species—the Columbian white-tailed deer. This species is easily observed and photographed from an asphalt driving/hiking/cycling trail around the refuge's perimeter. Evenings and mornings are the best times to visit. There's a high probability of seeing deer and elk year-round.

THE *TOURIST* COMES HOME

When you're a tourist, you usually travel new territory but not *Tourist No. 2* and for folks who remember ferry travel as an everyday event across the Columbia River near Astoria, the summer of 2016 provided a great reason to celebrate, perhaps even to shout it out from the Astoria rooftops: "The *Tourist* has come home!" The old ferry has done a lot in her near century of life but she has made her way back to Astoria, after 50 years—restored and reinstated to the place she first called home (astoriaferry.com; 503-836-3549).

Dulcye Taylor is part of a group of Astorians who brought the *Tourist No. 2* back home and she said holding on to history is "important to locals. We are the oldest settlement west of the Rockies and we are proud of distinctions like that. Some people think we're crazy to bring the *Tourist* home, but we're willing to accept that!"

Tourist No. 2 was a part of a ferry fleet built by Captain S. F. "Fritz" Elving in the 1920s. Elving started with the *Tourist No. 1* in 1921, following up with the *Tourist No. 2* in 1924 and the *Tourist No. 3* shortly after to keep up with demand.

She served passengers and traffic on the 9-mile round-trip between Astoria and Megler, Washington. More notable—she was a decorated minelaying vessel during WWII and protected the mouth of the Columbia River.

The Astoria-Megler Bridge opened in 1966, making the entire ferry service obsolete, scattering Elving's ferries throughout the world. Today, *Tourist No. 2* is the last one remaining, looking to find its last port of call right where it began on the Lower Columbia River. From her old-growth fir construction to original brass hardware, *Tourist No. 2* remains something wonderful to behold. Her new skipper is Captain Bruce Faling, and he said she handles like a dream. He was most impressed with her smooth ride. "She's very stable on a day like this but that's no surprise—she was built right here to handle the mighty Columbia River's ever-changing character. Plus, things can change in a heartbeat out here with wind, rain, and severe weather—but so far, so good."

"I think there's a number of people who have an emotional tie to this ferry," said Taylor—a member of the Astoria Ferry Group. "It's like they become the small children that rode this ferry when they were 6 to 10 years old." "I remember as a kid, riding across to Megler," added Bob Waldron, board member of the Oregon Maritime Museum. "Mom and Dad loved to dig clams on Long Beach and the ferry was part of the trip—it was the way you got around and it continues to be a touchstone for Oregon history buffs—this is about as good as it gets."

40A Wheatland Ferry Dock, *Daniel Matheny*

Where: Wheatland Road NW, Salem, OR 97304; 45.095267,-123.067154
Web: wheatlandferry.cccvc.com
Phone: 503-588-7979

40B Wahkiakum County Ferry, *Oscar B*

Where: 91499 Westport Ferry Road, Clatskanie, OR 97016
Web: www.co.wahkiakum.wa.us/depts/pw
Phone: 360-795-3301; 877-795-3910 (automated recording if ferry isn't running)

40c Julia Butler Hansen National Wildlife Refuge

Where: Cathlamet, WA 98612
Web: fws.gov/refuge/julia_butler_hansen
Phone: 360-795-3915

Watch the Episode: traveloregon.com/OregonFerries

February

41

Kilchis Point Reserve

If you know where to look, there are some chapters of Oregon history that come to life in the great outdoors. In Tillamook County, you can discover much about Native American heritage along a trail built by a community that celebrates its past. Kilchis Point Reserve is about as grassroots as it gets and Gary Albright's small army of volunteers have built miles of trails to prove it. "Ah, this place is so wonderful," said Albright, the director of the Tillamook County Pioneer Museum and leader of the effort to restore the unique 200-acre site. "We will have a couple dry days and then get a wet day and the flora and fauna take on a whole new look. When visitors walk the Kilchis Point Trail it just takes their breath away. We have visitors who never get outdoors and just get teary-eyed from the beauty of this place."

It's unlike any trail you've ever traveled—with old-growth spruce trees and tidal churned creeks and lush wetlands always by your side. With imagination, a hike along the Kilchis Point Trail also touches Oregon's distant past. Kilchis Point Reserve is the namesake for a community-based restoration project that began in 2011. The site encompasses 200 acres of county-owned forest and wetland property that hugs the eastern shore of Tillamook Bay near Bay City, Oregon.

Two hundred years ago it was the hub of a Salish Indian culture that may have arrived a thousand years earlier. Albright said the view to the place would have been much different back then: "You would see long cedar buildings—20 by 60 feet— and then smaller buildings scattered around the site. The nearby streams would be clogged with salmon and there would be waterfowl and shellfish available too. You would not walk more than a hundred yards to find food. Plus, it never froze and it never got too hot. I think it would have been a magical land."

The 2-mile-long Kilchis Point Trail includes boardwalks over wetlands that keep your feet dry.

You can better understand and appreciate this piece of Oregon paradise and learn more about the people who inhabited it when you step inside the newly remodeled Tillamook County Pioneer Museum. There are many ancient artifacts on display and Albright boasts that there are more than 50,000 artifacts in the museum's care. He said the collection is constantly growing too! "Every single day, someone comes in with a donation that has been in the family for decades—something they found on the site—but now they want it to be cared for by us." In addition to its numerous exhibits, the museum houses a library and genealogy research center; it is open every day except Mondays and major holidays and children under 10 are admitted free. You can pick up brochures at the museum's front desk for a self-guided tour of Tillamook's historic buildings (or download from tcpm.org/tchs.htm).

Albright can also explain how it was that a society of people—numbering in the thousands for hundreds and hundreds of years—seemingly disappeared overnight: "Between 1805 and 1851, the number of Salish people went from 2,200 to about 400 but they weren't losing people in wars. They weren't even fighting with the white settlers . . . it wasn't conflict, it was disease! The people were decimated by European diseases."

Back out on the 2-mile-long Kilchis Point Trail, Albright explained that the museum and the reserve go hand in hand as learning experiences that he hopes more people will try: "We tell the story there and then we bring it forward here and hope people come and enjoy both the indoor and outdoor wonder." Visitors Cindy

Grimmett and Donna Houston said they were amazed by the "wonder of it all." "You'd think you've died and gone to heaven," noted Grimmett. "This is gorgeous and totally natural and fantastic and you might see a bald eagle."

In fact, chances are you will see many eagles on a day that is too nice to stay indoors. Chances are you will also be struck by the silence of the place—the quiet can seem deafening and yet the trail is only a stone's throw from the small burg of Bay City. "I come here and all my troubles melt away," said Albright, who admits that he is an unabashed fan and enthusiastic leader of the grandest natural area in Tillamook County. "When you consider the human activity that occurred here for countless generations, this place is hallowed ground. I feel honored to be taking care of it and protecting it for future generations." The ⅓-mile Trailhead Loop is paved, ADA accessible, and lined with interpretive signs that will give you a real sense of the history of this place as well as the present-day natural habitats. Both the museum and reserve are popular destinations for school-group field trips. You can download an activity guide (and the answers) for your visit from tcpm.org/kilchispoint.htm (scroll down to the bottom of the page).

The remarkable volunteer effort to restore and enhance Kilchis Point Reserve never ends and Albright is always on the lookout for new volunteers who wish to take care of the site. In fact, a new bird-watching blind is in the works and eventually a Native American cedar longhouse will be built on the reserve to help tell the story of the native peoples who lived there. Students and adults have been instrumental in developing and maintaining the facility for everyone's enjoyment. Contact the museum if you are interested in volunteering for a future work party.

41A Kilchis Point Reserve

Where: US Highway 101 and Warren Street (continue on Warren to Spruce Street; trailhead is at corner of Spruce and Warren) Bay City, OR 97107

Web: tcpm.org/kilchispoint.htm; kilchispoint.wordpress.com

Phone: 503-842-4553

41B Tillamook County Pioneer Museum

Where: 2106 Second Street, Tillamook, OR 97141

Web: tcpm.org

Phone: 503-842-4553

Watch the Episode: traveloregon.com/KilchisPointReserve

42

Beauty Beyond Belief

I often go searching for islands of serenity at this time of year—places in Oregon that are special, scenic, and largely quiet where I can slow down, take a deep breath and, even for a short time, leave all my troubles behind, like the lovely little creek that invites hikers anytime on an easy 2-mile looped trail that brings the visitor face-to-face with gorgeous waterfalls. Photographers Lijah and Gabby Hanley chase the light for their perfect shots. The Northwest newlyweds—just out of their teens—share a passion for Oregon's outdoors. We joined them for a hike and a shoot along in a parkland I'd never been: Linn County's McDowell Creek Falls. "We are always looking for those off-the-beaten-path photographs,"

A large staircase brings you to creekside for a stunning view to Majestic Falls.

Lijah and Gabby Hanley "chase the light" for their perfect shots.

said young Lijah with a beaming smile. "I'm always trying to get something new."

Despite the calendar, sunshine played peekaboo, where Majestic Falls—one of several waterfalls in the park—puts on quite a bone-chilling show. Lijah even stepped knee-deep in the creek so as to frame just the right shot. "It is cold out here," he admitted. "But you know, you have to be in the water to get the foreground. It's pretty rare when we find a spot that's totally unique that we haven't seen yet. This is certainly that and a whole lot more."

Gabby added: "We have a bond because we both enjoy getting out—anywhere—and shooting together does that for us. Plus, we run a business together and that's been really rewarding." That much is certain—Lijah picked up his first camera at age 9—and it was a leftover from his mother's own portrait photography business. From that moment on, he said he was hooked.

"It was awesome! It was my mom's old Canon Rebel and I fixed the broken shutter and started shooting pretty much anything in my backyard. From bugs to flowers and anything else that might be around the house. It soon became an excuse to go on longer adventures and explore the Northwest."

At 13, Lijah Hanley won a *National Geographic* photo contest and the prize included an all-expense-paid trip with a professional photographer to Machu Picchu in Peru. It was a fine start for a young man on the fast track to become one of the region's best. He continues to relish the opportunity to travel and shoot anywhere anytime of the year.

Gabby is always by his side—in fact, the two just returned from a near year-long honeymoon; during that time, they shot thousands of images across thirty-eight states. "As much as we love the Northwest," said Lijah, "there is so much of the world to see—any chance we get to go exploring, we jump on it."

His images are beautiful and often show a piercing light that shoots across the scene and seems magical—and yet, it feels just right too. "It's true," said Lijah. "We are chasing the light more than we are chasing the landscape itself. It's the light that makes the images—absolutely."

Both agree that 60-acre McDowell Creek County Park offers a certain beauty beyond belief where streamside conifers and moss-draped maples complete a setting that is classic Oregon rain forest. "For us to capture the essence of a place in an image," added Gabby, "and have people see our image and say, 'Wow—I know that place—it feels like home.' For us to bring that feeling to our viewers, it's just a really wonderful thing that keeps us doing our work. We love it!"

McDowell Creek Falls has 3 miles of well-marked hiking trails suitable even for young children (and your dog on a leash), but use caution as some areas can be muddy and slippery around the falls. Also be aware that the loop trail crosses the road twice so be sure children stay close to an adult for safety. There are stairs throughout, but if you take the larger loop in a clockwise direction, you'll traverse down the final large staircase. Restrooms and a picnic area are also available. Your family will relish beautiful views of the falls from bridges and viewing decks. And remember to bring your camera!

---

42 McDowell Creek Park

Where: 43170 McDowell Creek Drive, Lebanon, OR 97355

Web: linnparks.com/parks/mcdowell-creek-falls

Phone: 541-967-3917

Watch the Episode: traveloregon.com/McDowellCreek

43

Higher Education—
High Desert Museum

It's funny how some of the best surprises are often found right in your own backyard. So it is from the eastern Cascades point of view where elbow room is measured by the wide-open vistas of snow-shrouded landscapes; the kinds of scenes that capture your heart and may lead you to wonder aloud: "Why have I never traveled this way before?" It is a question on many visitors' minds at a place where the answer is easy to find and higher education is center stage at the High Desert Museum near Bend. You'll agree with the staff's adage that this remarkable complex of displays, demonstrations, and hands-on events make the museum "more like an expedition than an exhibition."

According to former museum spokesperson Dana Whitelaw, the museum examines and explains the natural history and the special qualities of high desert life: "They may have seen the sign on the highway for years and finally stopped in and people on a regular basis are blown away by how much is here. They experience so much of the West through art, cultural and natural history, and the wildlife. We are proud that we can be that relevant."

The high desert is also referred to as the Intermountain West—a region bordered on the east by the Rockies and on the west by the Cascades/Sierras. It includes the Columbia and Snake River plateaus to the north and the Great Basin to the south. This is big sky country—roomy and remote and very rugged! Anchored by towering mountains, the high desert distances are great and striking for their seeming nothingness. From sage and juniper plains to aspen bordered meadows, the mix of mountains, serrated rimrock canyons, and softly contoured slopes reach into cool streams and lakes. It is a lonesome place that can make the heart soar for soulful qualities and silent moments. In fact, solitude is easy to come by in between the tiny hamlets and far-flung cattle spreads that are often the only marks of human activity.

The museum examines and explains the natural history and the special qualities of high desert life very well. From birds of prey, such as hawks and eagles, to river otters and porcupines, this is a place where you can see and learn about the arid Intermountain West, which includes portions of eight Western states and the Canadian province of British Columbia. The museum spreads across 150 acres filled with exhibits and demonstrations. A mile-long trail goes through 20 acres of trailside exhibits, including a trout stream, otter ponds, porcupine dens, and historic interpretive displays of frontier life and industry.

The museum offers educational opportunities for all ages including kids' camps scheduled on days off from school and Backpack Explorers—a special hands-on experience for children ages 3 to 5 that takes them on a journey through exhibits and trails and even provides take-home activities (preregistration is required). Or go online to find a daily schedule of presentations, guided hikes, interactive discussions, and up-close wildlife encounters (highdesertmuseum.org/daily-schedule). You can also plan ahead with guided learning activities and worksheets (highdesertmuseum.org/learning-materials).

Oregon's High Desert Museum offers kids' camps scheduled on days off from school.

Everyone can lend a hand feeding the wildlife at the High Desert Museum.

A favorite destination for children is inside the Earl A. Chiles Center: the walking tour through vignettes of life called Spirit of the West. This timeline stroll covers thousands of years in the span of a few hundred feet. Along the way, you are invited into a Native American campsite to learn how hardy vegetation, abundant wildlife, and a mineral-rich terrain sustained generations of natives. Then come the explorers and the fur trappers, the miners and sheepherders and sodbusters, and finally the immigrants, fresh off the Oregon Trail. All of this is explained through sights and sounds that put you in scenes from the Stone Age to rustic dirt roads in a Western frontier town. Few places convey the story of humans on the desert as well as this experience, including how the mines, then the ranches, and then the railroads brought more and more people to the desert, so that by the 1880s, small cottage industries began to sprout and, in many ways, forever change the face of the desert.

Other risk takers of the same era included countless homesteaders like Mrs. Blair (portrayed in full costume by local volunteer Linda Evans), who help you to see and understand how tough life was in the high desert as you stroll through her replica farmstead from the 1880s. She admitted that the hardest part of all was, "Loneliness, because we're 40 miles from Prineville and it takes 2 days to get there. I go maybe four or five times a year. So we do get lonely and the children keep us busy, but I dearly love to have visitors."

You'll love seeing the many wildlife species on display at the museum too. Hawks, eagles, and turkey vultures are frequently seen soaring over the wide expanse of the desert, but at the museum you can see them all close at hand and learn about their special adaptations for survival. "When it's behind a screen or behind glass, you're so removed," noted wildlife curator Nolan Harvey. "But when you're up close you can see the feathers move, you see the bird move and pay attention to you, and hopefully makes you want to know more about the animal and gives you that bond."

The close connection with wildlife is a lasting legacy message from the museum's founder, Donald Kerr, who owned a passion for wildlife and was a big believer that animals can connect with newcomers and perhaps change attitudes about the high desert. "We're very proud that all the animals you see here were either captive born or they have been through rehabilitation and cannot be released," added Harvey. "Our wildlife get a second chance at life to educate the rest of us." Whether you're seeking education or recreation, the High Desert Museum is not to be missed and will bring you back time and again. "It's a real jewel," noted Dana Whitelaw. "A true treasure of Central Oregon!" The museum is open every day except Thanksgiving, Christmas, and New Year's Day and children age 4 and under are admitted free. It will open your eyes, your mind, and perhaps your heart to a region that has often been overlooked.

---

43 High Desert Museum

Where: 59800 South Highway 97, Bend, OR 97702

Web: highdesertmuseum.org

Phone: 541-382-4754

Watch the Episode: traveloregon.com/highdesertmuseum

44

Indoor Kite Flying

W hen the winter weather turns wicked, step indoors at the Oregon Soccer Center in Clackamas, Oregon, and discover serenity and soul-satisfying rewards *flying a kite*! A Kite? Indoors? Oh yes, it's been a terrific source of exercise and soothing therapy for kids and adults alike the past 4 decades. And there's more—it turns out that Oregon is home to some of the finest kite-flying talent in the world. Many Oregon fliers travel the Pacific Northwest to perform and some are even world travelers!

"Kites *can* be flown indoors," insisted Brett Morris, director of the Western Region of the American Kitefliers Association (kite.org), who hosted my recent visit to the Soccer Center—the weekly gathering place for local indoor fliers. In fact, indoor kite flying and competition are becoming more and more popular all the time "with performers appearing on shows like *America's Got Talent*," said Morris. "Indoor kites are designed to fly in a windless environment. It's a type of kite principally designed for indoor use, but can also be flown outdoors when light wind would make traditional kite flying impossible."

Indoor kites are flown by using the relative wind provided by the motion of the kite flier, pulling the sail against the still air in a room. The fliers create their own lift by slowly walking backwards, walking in large circles, and occasionally pulling on the line. "It takes practice," according to longtime flier Wayne Dowler. "But the indoor kite can be flown through all angles around the flier, including directly overhead on a single line!" It's a relatively short-line form of flying that demands a certain level of finesse. It is addicting to some, funny looking to others, but I suspect it's reasonably cool for most kite fliers.

Indoor kites are flown using the wind created by the motion of the kite flier.

Many folks, like Morris and Dowler, said that they come to indoor kite flights for the exercise. "You're out here moving and sweating—you're exercising and getting your daily run—for me, it's that and increased confidence too," said Dowler. The kites are so sensitive to air movements that they can actually be affected by someone else walking around nearby, and for experienced fliers like US National Champion John Barresi, the overall effect is graceful and artistic. I watch wide-eyed as Barresi's agile movements included flying his quad kite (four different lines that control flight as he provides the lift) while lying down on the floor as he made the kite jump and scoot and zoom just inches above the floor. He was a pro in action and made the sport look easy and beautiful! "When people fly, they're showing the better part of themselves," said Barresi. "Your chin is up, you're looking up, and your heart is open and you're playing with this tension in the line. Your mind goes calm. You don't have to change your religion or your diet or anything to be a great kite flier."

Morris pointed out the number of youngsters who were also flying their own kites and noted, "They can make or buy them, but one thing is for sure: they love the exercise and challenge of keeping their very own kites up in the air and doing tricks too." He said that the sport or recreation (which is it?) takes us all back to our childhoods when we built newspaper or garbage bag kites and learned to fly them. "It's so rewarding to see a youngster fly something they had a hand in building."

Kites are also used for therapy, according to Paul Burks. He is a firefighter with the Hoodland Fire Department near Mt. Hood and in 2013, he suffered what he called a "super concussion." A fire hose with a brass fitting hit him on the head and he said the result was devastating. "I went from being firefighter and honor guard commander and flying outdoor kites to the point that I couldn't even walk. An accident like mine steals your entire life away."

Indeed, the accident turned Burks's physical and emotional well-being upside down, but he insisted that learning to fly a small plastic kite made a huge difference in his recovery. "The nice thing is that these kites move slow enough that if you're having overload problems like me—sensory overload—you can keep up with this small kite. Post-traumatic stress disorders, balance problems, brain injuries, limb loss, stroke—even folks in wheelchairs, I've worked with them all during my own recovery and I have watched people successfully fly kites and gain confidence and see the return of their motor skills. Kites are magical!"

Folks of all ages can learn how it's done through the American Kitefliers Association and join in the fun each week at the Oregon Soccer Center. So consider going indoors the next time someone tells you, "Go fly a kite!"

---

44 Oregon Soccer Center

Where: 17015 SE 82nd Drive, Clackamas, OR 97015
Web: oscindoor.com
Phone: 503-655-7529
Watch the Episode: traveloregon.com/IndoorKites

March

45

Marine Discovery Tours

The Oregon coast is a place where carefree moments are easy to come by and can make you feel young all over. One place in particular—Yaquina Bay at Newport— offers a perspective to the marine world that's unique and educational. Don and Fran Mathews own and operate Marine Discovery Tours (MDT), and the centerpiece of their ecotourism business is *Discovery,* a 65-foot boat that's as much a floating science laboratory as it is a retired fishing craft. Marine Discovery Tours specializes in trips that teach visitors more about the ocean, the estuary, and all the marine life that can be found there. "We have travelers come from all over the world," noted Fran. "And they're here to find the real Oregon coast. Well, we can offer that—we have our beautiful 4,000-acre Yaquina Bay and 12 miles of Yaquina River too—plus—the big blue Pacific Ocean is just off Newport's front step."

Fran's husband, Don Mathews, is a former commercial fisherman who ranged across the Pacific all the way to the Bering Sea before settling at Newport. He noted, "After all of my travels, it makes me feel quite grateful that I'm able to work and live and play on the Oregon coast." Who wouldn't feel grateful on a sun-kissed day where a rising tide found skipper Don steering *Discovery* across the bay for a typical 2-hour exploration of the estuary. Fran observed that her "class," thirty-three folks of all ages from all across the country—had one thing on their minds: "Oh, people just want to do stuff—and so we have them pulling crab pots, pulling plankton nets, visiting with our naturalist, chatting with Don in the wheelhouse, and even driving the boat." And on their Sea Life Cruise, children age 3 and under ride for free.

The Mathewses have been guiding visitors across the bay for almost 20 years. They were the first to try their hands at ecotourism in Newport and it has really taken

"All hands on deck" for hands-on science includes learning about
Dungeness crabs aboard Marine Discovery Tours.

off for them—and even for longtime local residents who learn something new. "We have Oregonians who live on the coast who've never been out on the ocean," said Fran. "And it's such an eye-opener for them to see home from the opposite direction instead of always being on land and looking out."

Steven Mulvey, the MDT's official onboard naturalist, added that it's also an experience that puts people to work—but in a fun way! "All hands on deck for hands-on science," said Mulvey. He retrieved a 30-foot length of rope floating off the starboard side of the *Discovery.* The rope was tied to a submerged crab pot. As he handed the rope to one of the guests, he said, "Pull, pull, pull!"

Soon the trap appeared at the surface and Mulvey hoisted it aboard. Inside the crab trap, a half-dozen Dungeness crabs scurried across the wire mesh bottom. "Okay, folks—we hit the jackpot—lots of crab here—who wants to hold a Dungeness crab?" he yelled to the crowd. Several tentative hands went up and each person had a chance to hold and examine a crab up close as Mulvey explained, "A female Dungeness will release about a million eggs per crab per season. Now, that's productivity! The ocean affects everything. It affects the climate. It affects our food—where our food comes from—and so it is really important to protect it and understand it."

Fran watched the activity on the back deck and added, "Our best day every day is to get people out on our boat and let them feel like they own a part of all of this. Because we really do! Look at this beautiful waterway. This belongs to all of us—don't you think we should learn all we can about it?" Nearby, there's another destination that may help you to answer Fran's question.

I am a big believer that learning more about the places that I visit is critically important to appreciating all that Oregon has to offer. So in Newport I regularly stop in at the Hatfield Marine Science Center (HMSC). Located on the south side of Yaquina Bay, just off US Highway 101, the center is one of the best bargains of the entire area. Hatfield MSC is a professional science base that is the home for scores of scientists linked with Oregon State University (OSU).

The exhibit areas of the center are open to the public and admission is free, although donations are accepted and appreciated. The center is like a window to the ocean with exhibits that display the varied marine species that are found just off Oregon's coastal shore. Your kids can experiment with the science of nature at the hands-on erosion tank and tsunami wave tank, or get up close to sea creatures in the tide pool touch tanks. In March, the center hosts a Winter Whale Watch Week with programming, exhibits, and activities that center around the gray whales migrating along Oregon's coast. Bill Hanshumaker, HMSC's retired education director, explained, "I think the animals are the big attractor, and my challenge is to enhance the learning that takes place with hands-on activities, talks, lectures . . . we're helping expand the knowledge of the people that walk through the door and I promise—you will not be bored!"

Throughout the year, the center conducts other educational programs including 2-hour family sessions in July (for families with children age 4 and older), 4-day-long summer day camps for kids 8 to 18, marine science career days for high schoolers, and lab and field classes for groups of students pre-K through adult. And be sure to check out OSU's Oregon Coast Quests any time of the year—fun, clue-directed hunts in various parks and locations along the coast (hmsc.oregonstate.edu/quests).

---

45 Marine Discovery Tours

Where: 345 SW Bay Boulevard, Newport, OR 97365
Web: marinediscovery.com
Phone: 800-903-BOAT or 541-265-6200

Hatfield Marine Science Center

Where: 2030 SE Marine Science Drive, Newport, OR 97365
Web: hmsc.oregonstate.edu
Phone: 541-867-0100

Watch the Episode: traveloregon.com/marinescience

46

Shellburg Falls Hike

Tucked into the foothills of the Oregon Cascades, Silver Falls State Park is the perfect place for building lasting memories. "You've got the geology—the waterfalls—that's why most of us are here, that's why I'm here, why you're here—why there's a park at all," noted longtime Park Ranger Dorothy Brown-Kwaiser. "If you're a first-time visitor, I say come here first—the South Falls Lodge area. If you're up for a long hike, go down into the canyon where you get into the park's wilderness."

Wilderness-like experiences are easy to come by in this part of the Oregon Cascades. In fact, take the short 8-mile-long drive from Lyons, Oregon, into the nearby Santiam State Forest and discover a place where the silence shouts at you. I've been looking forward to this visit to Shellburg Falls, sort of a second cousin to Silver Falls State Park, which is—as the crow flies—just a few miles away. The access is easy and offers a short hike to a beautiful waterfall.

The main trail to Shellburg Falls takes you behind the falls into a large natural grotto.

Shellburg Falls is the centerpiece waterfall in the small sliver of state forest along Stout Creek Canyon. For this hike, head down the single-track Shellburg Falls Trail for about 0.7 mile to reach the falls. A short side trail leads to a viewpoint near the base of the falls and the main trail circles behind the waterfall in a large natural grotto.

What a beauty Shellburg Falls is: a 100-foot plunge over a protruding basalt ledge that creates a large recess behind the falls called the amphitheater. The hike to this falls makes for a relaxing afternoon, particularly with children or inexperienced hikers. The trail actually takes you behind the falls for a (sometimes wet and muddy) spectacular view of the falls. And there's more—a small, quiet seven-site campground allows an overnight stay (with picnic tables, barbecue grills, and restrooms)—a fine way to spend a weekend any time of year.

While the day-use area is closed in winter months, you can access the trail all year. According to the Oregon Department of Forestry, drive 25 miles east from Salem to Lyons, Oregon. Once reaching Lyons take Fern Ridge Road northbound and drive 1.2 miles. Drive until you reach a yellow gate on the east side of the road; an information sign is located near the yellow gate. Vehicles may be parked in the space near the gate. Please make sure the gate is not blocked so that fire and emergency vehicles will have access. From the yellow gate hike 1.2 miles over a gravel road to reach Shellburg Falls. This road is on private land and visitors must stay on the roadway. After walking 1.2 miles you will find a small bridge with a waterfall below it: this is the lower Shellburg Falls. The lower Shellburg Falls Trailhead is located here, and a trail sign gives directions to the upper Shellburg Falls.

46A Silver Falls State Park

Where: 20024 Silver Falls Highway SE, Sublimity, OR 97385
Web: oregonstateparks.org
Phone: 503-873-8681; 800-551-6949

46B Shellburg Falls/Santiam State Forest

Where: Fern Ridge Road SE, Lyons, OR 97358
Web: oregon.gov/ODF; oregon.gov/ODF/Documents/Recreation/
SantiamStateForestRecreationGuide.pdf
Phone: 503-859-2151

Watch the Episode: traveloregon.com/ShellburgFalls

47

Wildlife Safari—
Lions and Tigers and Bears

March spring vacations always put a little extra spring in my step! When my sons were in grade school, it was the anticipation of a new adventure and the chance to experience the outdoors through their eyes that motivated me to pack up a bit of our household and take our home on the road. That's especially true when I had a new destination in mind that might teach the youngsters about wildlife. For more than 40 years, Wildlife Safari in a unique Southern Oregon setting has done just that for tens of thousands of families. The wildlife park spans more than 600 acres of rolling, oak-studded hills and savanna-like grasslands near the small burg of Winston. As you travel through Winston, you cannot miss the centerpiece of the town: a life-sized bronze sculpture of the rare cheetah, an endangered species that numbers but a few thousand in the wild. The statue serves as a symbol of the continuing efforts that Wildlife Safari established many years ago to help wildlife.

This parkland is very special, not only for the more than 1,000 animals that live there (some rarely seen outside their home ranges or even at city zoos), but because the visitors are in the cages—not the animals. Perhaps *cage* is a bit of a stretch, for you actually drive through this spread-out park in the comfort of your car. It's the kind of place made for family enjoyment, according to Dot Irvin, a former member of the park staff, who told me that people get excited about seeing wildlife in this unusual setting "not only for the closeness you get to the animals, but the chance to learn more about them, too."

Wildlife curator Sarah Roy said, "It's the opposite of a zoo because you drive through in your car, and a giraffe can walk right up to your car, rhinos can walk

Visitors can experience wildlife encounters that put you up close and face-to-face with brown bears.

right up to your car, the zebra herd will run across the road. It's amazing!" Roy was right! Just like that—our interview came to a halt as J. T., a towering 12-year-old giraffe stopped, stooped, and zoomed in for a closer look. Actually, there were many similar incidents and that's not surprising when you consider there are 300 different species . . . close to 1,000 animals "in charge" at a park that's unlike any you've been to before. Our trip offered something that visitors can experience called Wildlife Encounters. It's a new program that puts you in closer proximity to many species—a bit of what Roy called, "behind the scenes opportunities." We visited the brown bear area and found ourselves just feet away from a trio of 6-year-old brown bears—separated by half a dozen electrically charged so-called "hot wires."

Roy explained, "The boys just woke up from hibernation a week ago and we come out here several times a day to do training. Bears are so smart and mentally active so we give them simple fruit juices that are frozen and the bears treat them like popsicles. We also offer fruit trays and nuts or hide berries in boxes so they get a chance to rip them apart and play a little bit. We scatter treats around the area, throw frozen fruit in the pond, and they love it." Note that for some of the wildlife encounters you will need to make reservations in advance and depending on the encounter, a minimum age limit may apply.

There's nearly 4 miles of roadway that wind through the complex on a route that takes you through several distinct animal communities including Asia, Africa,

Wildlife Safari offers picture perfect-moments, so be sure to have your camera or cell phone on hand.

and the Americas. Each area is home to scores of species you rarely get to see this close. Flamingos, cougars, emus, tigers—and each is fascinating. Nearby, we stopped in for a rare encounter with a pair of animals that have grown up together. Ellie is an Anatolian shepherd dog and her enclosure friend is a cheetah named Sonora. Each is 4 years old and they have grown up together. "The dog breed is quite protective, loyal, and dedicated," explained Roy. "To whatever they are raised with, so basically Sonora is Ellie's herd of sheep. We wanted to bring this breed in as a companion animal to teach more about saving cheetahs in the wild."

As we slowly motored along the paved roadway, I was struck by how often we'd be at arm's length from many exotic critters I'd seen behind bars in zoos or on television. In fact, in the Africa area, we were suddenly stopped by a pair of stubborn ostriches, who, like dutiful traffic cops, had taken up position smack in the middle of the road and wouldn't budge an inch. Then they moved toward our car and began to peck away at the windshield. This brought on a raucous, rowdy chorus of laughter from my sons, who'd never seen such a sight. We were baffled and couldn't understand their behavior. Roy then pointed out that the giant birds were actually eating the bugs that had taken up permanent, fatal residence on the car's windshield. "Oh, it happens all the time," she laughed. "This pair's a real hit with the visitors—quite an act, huh?"

"I'll say," my young Kevin noted. And with a giggle he added, "They must think we're the blue plate special."

After an hour or so, we arrived back at Safari Village, near the park's entrance, where you may stroll around the manicured lawns, neatly trimmed hedges, masses of blooming daylilies, and carefully trimmed shade trees of Safari Village Gardens. The gardens play the major role in setting the atmosphere and help provide a tolerable microclimate in Southern Oregon's often sweltering summer heat, especially after a drive through the park in a car without air-conditioning. The Safari Village offers an air-conditioned restaurant where you can get a fine meal, a snack bar for your favorite soft drink and light lunch, a gift shop for memorabilia, and regular educational animal shows. It's so comfortable and so inviting, you may not wish to leave, but you'll miss more interesting parts of the parkland.

If the village is not to your liking, a number of benches are strategically located beneath ample shade trees next to ponds of water where you can watch the pink flamingos. Ah yes, the pink flamingo, practically an icon in America's landscape, except that these are not plastic; they are very real and happy to pose for you in front of bright yellow daylilies and a shimmering pool.

As my family took advantage of the colorful photo opportunity, I sat and chatted with Dot Irvin to learn more about Wildlife Safari's cheetah icon. She explained that the cheetah has been the park's symbol from the beginning because the graceful cats face such terrible odds against their survival in the wild. Only 7,100 cheetahs remain in Africa countries. The plight of cheetahs symbolizes the problems that many predators face throughout the world. As Irvin explained, "Many people fear predators, especially big cats such as the lion, cheetah, and leopard. We are often taught to fear carnivores without understanding their unique behaviors and essential roles in healthy ecosystems. Our attitudes and misconceptions have led to their endangerment because what people fear they often choose to destroy."

Wildlife Safari tries to change that attitude by helping you to understand and care about wildlife. Perhaps that will improve their chance of survival in the wild. Roy noted that in the wild, cheetahs remain critically endangered. But it's the king of the animal kingdom that you may remember the most. I will certainly never forget our encounter with Tao, a 3-year-old African male lion. You see, we played tug-of-war with him. Two towering fences separate the lion from humans—each grabs hold of the 40-foot-long rope—humans with their hands, Tao with claws and powerful jaws and sharp teeth. We then pulled back and forth on the long rope—or rather we held our ground while Tao pulled on us. It was a remarkable experience as the 400-pound lion showed his amazing strength and easily pulled on the rope that six of us held on to.

"It is good exercise and the animals seem to have fun. So do the people," noted Roy. "Each looks forward to this exercise—in fact, our lions come running over anytime it is rope time. It's pretty impressive when you feel him pulling—you can really feel that power in the rope—it's amazing!"

It is all of that—and more —and contributes to a remarkable outdoor experience across fascinating parkland that will entertain and teach you much about wildlife across the planet.

During summer months, the park provides several opportunities for families to camp out overnight—the Safari Adventure Camp includes plenty of free time in the village along with a nocturnal animal show and a guided night hike followed by a special animal encounter in the morning. Several 4-day summer day camps are available for children ages 4 to 11. If your 11- to 17-year-old child is available to volunteer during summer months, they can apply to the park's Junior Zookeeper program and help in a variety of settings including the petting zoo, summer camps, animal husbandry and presentations, village booths, and special events. Three one-month sessions are available in June, July, and August. Be sure to register for all these activities online.

---

47 Wildlife Safari

Where: 1790 Safari Road, Winston, OR 97496
Web: wildlifesafari.net
Phone: 541-679-6761
Watch the Episode: ttraveloregon.com/wildlifesafari

Coos Bay History and Vanishing Wilderness

The beauty of Oregon's coastal ports is that they often shine like faceted jewels throughout the seasons. I favor these quaint ports of call as I have a passion for traveling through them. I believe that's due, in part, to the pride that many local folks have shared with me from their corners of the state. For example, Marty Giles loves to brag about the love affair she has with her hometown of Coos Bay. "We have lovely weather year-round! It might be wet at times in the spring-time, but never bone-chilling cold." Marty added there's simply so much to do along the southern Oregon coast and you don't travel far from Coos Bay to find it. At each turn, there's a unique adventure waiting to be revealed.

On a recent spring afternoon, Marty guided me to see a new development on the Coos Bay waterfront called simply the Coos History Museum. The $10 million, 13,000-square-foot museum is what Marty nicknamed the "People's Museum," because its fifteen rotating exhibits are filled with stories from the people who lived the history. The museum is open Tuesdays through Sundays; the entry fee for children ages 5 to 17 is modest and children under age 5 are admitted free. Every second Sunday the museum hosts Family Fun Day with free admission for all and special hands-on activities for children. Their teacher resources for fourth- and fifth-grade students are available on their website and might also be of interest to parents. "We need to rethink how to use our waterfront, and this is the beginning of that," added Marty. "That's the one reason why this project is so important, for it's kind of reclaiming the town's waterfront from the leftovers of severely diminished logging and fishing industries."

The southern Oregon coastline is a remote place and in Coos County

The $10 million Coos History Museum features exhibits from the people who lived local history.

it rises from sea level to 3,500 feet. The Coos Bay estuary is a semi-enclosed, elongated series of sloughs and tidewater streams that drains approximately 825 square miles of southern Oregon's rugged Coast Range. The county has long been home to a collection of working people at a far remove from help. "They're not on the I-5 corridor, so they've had to do things for themselves and work hard for what they have," explained Marty.

Marty introduced me to Frank Smoot, spokesperson for the Coos History Museum, who quickly let me know that the town's newest museum is worth your time to visit because it offers visiting families stories about "assorted people and places" that are worth investigating along the coast. "If you want to know about the place—know the character of the place—then start your southern Oregon coast journey right here in this building," said Smoot, who quickly added that the museum's collections include more than 40,000 artifacts and over 200,000 photo images. "This is a great place to launch your adventures because you understand here what you're seeing and then go out to see it."

One such story on view through photos and oral descriptions is the ill-fated tale of a lumber ship called the *Czarina*, which wrecked near Coos Bay in 1910. Huge waves engulfed the hull and exhausted the vessel's steam engines. Unable to steer, the ship floundered and ended up sideways. Its cargo rolled into the ocean. "As soon as the waves came over the top of the boat, it set free the lumber," said Smoot. "There was no way to jump in the ocean because there were all of these logs floating around. As our old photos show, there were fewer and fewer men clinging to the rigging and only one man survived."

Marty noted that the connection with seafaring stories continues each year when tall ships visit Coos Bay (festofsailcoosbay.com). Two of these ships are the *Lady Washington,* a full-scale reproduction of the first American ship to sail the West Coast, and the *Hawaiian Chieftain,* a steel-hulled representation of trading vessels that plied the Hawaiian Islands during the late 1700s and early 1800s. "Each spring, visitors may tour the boats or even take an Adventure Sail, where they may participate in hoisting sails and other chores. This place is coming alive for adults and kids alike," added Marty. "It's really neat and travelers need to turn off Coastal Highway 101 and visit the Coos Bay waterfront."

When you step out of the new history museum, you don't walk very far to discover a Coos Bay "time capsule"; in fact, a short stroll across the street and you reach the fascinating Marshfield Sun Printing Museum. "You walk into a frontier newspaper and we're about the last one left in the country," noted museum curator Lionel Youst. "All the towns in the West would have had a newspaper like this, but this one may be the only one that is still intact and operational." Youst said that from 1890 to 1944, Jesse Allen Luse collected the local news and set the type and printed hundreds of copies of the weekly newspaper. When he died in 1944, the place was boarded up for nearly 30 years and then—when the city opened it up—they couldn't believe what they found. "The *Marshfield Sun* is intact with all the nineteenth-century printing equipment, the type cases, the presses—all in their original location and they all work," said a smiling Youst. The museum is open Tuesdays through Saturdays Memorial Day through Labor Day. Other visiting times may be available by appointment. Volunteers will gladly explain and demonstrate the presses and printing equipment. Admission is free, but donations are welcome. Back on the Coos Bay Boardwalk, Marty and I stood under cover from a spring rain shower as she offered that both museums are excellent complements to the many easy-to-reach outdoor destinations—and will help you better understand the people and the region.

A short drive from Coos Bay is a pristine corner of the coast known as the South Slough Estuarine Research Reserve (ERR), a sanctuary that encompasses more than 4,400 acres of upland forest, 115 acres of riparian habitat, and 800 acres of tidelands that have been federally protected since 1974. The site includes an interpretive center that is enjoyable for children of all ages, is open to the public Tuesdays through Saturdays, and houses exhibits, a video viewing area, a small bookstore, and facilities for formal lectures. They even host occasional craft-making and interactive activities for children as young as 1 year old. Be sure to explore their online event calendar to take advantage of these opportunities. An outdoor amphitheater located near the interpretive center serves as an area for presentations and also as a resting place for hikers. We hurried into the South Slough Visitor Center to beat an April downpour and Marty noted with a laugh, "People complain about the rain, but really there's no such thing as bad weather, just inappropriate clothing."

Inside the center, exhibits put you in touch with a rare piece of Oregon coastal environment, especially the aquaria with both freshwater and saltwater marine life. Education specialist Joy Tally said, "They help you experience what an estuary is—see what the habitats are—and then you use that as your jumping off point for exploring the rest of South Slough." There are more than 5,000 acres in South Slough Preserve—approximately 1,000 of that is the slough itself, and the rest is protected upland forest or marshland. You will find plenty of trails to explore at South Slough Preserve. "It is undisturbed, it is not developed, and you do have more interaction with wildlife here. It's quiet! It's peaceful! And you can picture what life was like many years ago across this southern branch of greater Coos Bay," noted Marty.

One of my favorite trails is Hidden Creek—a trail that offers a 2.3-mile round-trip hike that's fine for youngsters. It follows Hidden Creek from the interpretive center to the estuary's edge. The trail descends 300 feet to a boardwalk, which winds through freshwater and saltwater marshes. In addition, there are many stunning views along the trail, including those from atop a two-level deck that looks across a marsh area to the Winchester Arm of the slough. As we strolled, Marty showed us how estuaries form where freshwater flows from the land and mixes with the tidal flows of saltwater from the ocean. She pointed out that estuaries have a higher productivity than most other ecosystems on earth. Hidden Creek flows through the ground to a narrow stream channel before expanding into a freshwater swamp of red alder and skunk cabbage. It abounds with wildlife species including deer, elk, soaring bald eagles, plentiful waterfowl, and myriad shorebirds.

"One of the reasons South Slough is particularly inviting is because it is fairly pristine," said Marty. "It has high-quality marsh and tide flat that are largely unaffected by human activity. As a result, we have been the center of scientific research since our inception over 40 years ago."

In fact, more than 3,000 youngsters trek this trail each school year to gain a better understanding of natural science. The Research Reserve offers educational programs for school groups ages pre-K through twelfth grade. As Marty explained all of this, I was reminded how rare clean, undeveloped estuaries have become in Oregon. In fact, up to 70 percent of the state's coastal wetlands and marshes have been diked, then drained, then filled, and as a result, lost forever. The Hidden Creek Trail allows you to keep your feet dry as you amble along with gorgeous views at every turn. So be sure to bring your camera or cell phone to capture memories; I'm sure you'll agree that it is time well spent.

Note: During the summer, guided tours on the water are available. While the South Slough ERR does not offer boats for rent, it will provide a trained interpretive guide to describe the natural and cultural history along the 6-mile tour and a shuttle vehicle to transport drivers (participating paddlers) back to their vehicles at the put-in point. All participants are responsible for their own safety equipment, boats, and vehicles.

48A Coos History Museum

Where: 1210 N. Front Street, Coos Bay, OR 97420
Web: cooshistory.org
Phone: 541-756-6320

Marshfield Sun Printing Museum

Where: 1049 N. Front Street, Coos Bay, OR 97420
Web: marshfieldsunprintingmuseum.appspot.com
Phone: 541-267-3762

48B South Slough Estuarine Research Reserve

Where: 61907 Seven Devils Road, Charleston, OR 97420
Web: oregon.gov/DSL/SSNERR
Phone: 541-888-5558

Watch the Episode: traveloregon.com/SouthCoastDunes

Index

Printed in the USA
CPSIA information can be obtained
at www.ICGtesting.com
JSHW012025140824
68134JS00033B/2884

9 781513 260464